THE
MULTI-MILLION DOLLAR
MOMPRENEUR

*Your guide to business mastery,
uncommon freedom, & legacy wealth*

by Julie Roy

Published by: GWN Publishing
www.GWNPublishing.com

Cover Design: Kristina Conatser

ISBN: 978-1-959608-84-4 Print
          978-1-959608-85-1 Hardcover

DEDICATION

To my husband, my children, and our family and friends, whose unwavering support has been our ultimate foundation;

To my mentors, whose wisdom have illuminated my path; And to all those who dare to dream of a wealthier future,

May this book serve as a guide to your financial success and a legacy of prosperity for generations to come.

CONTENTS

FOREWORD

What Makes Me Tick!

My family background is 100 percent Italian. In fact, to this day, after dinner at my Nonna's house (she is 94, by the way), I still revert to being that "best granddaughter" I can be, by clearing the table while the rest of the family hangs out and has coffee, sambuca, and dessert. If I didn't get up and help do all the things, they would say (or at least think), "What's wrong with her? She's so lazy, is she okay?" Meanwhile, here I am, you know, just a wife, a mom of four, and running a few multi-million dollar companies in my spare time. Nope, I'm not kidding!

Looking at where I am now, people often assume I came from a family with money who bankrolled my success and made it easy for me to gain financial freedom. Not the case at all. I had a loving, generous, Italian family, so I never went hungry or without a home, but we did not have disposable income and I know my mother fought daily to make sure we had what we did. What I learned growing up, what was drilled into my head, was the idea that if you wanted something, you worked hard for it.

And work I did. I have been working since I was nine years old. As soon as I was old enough to be trusted with the responsibility, I babysat the neighborhood kids. I also got a job at a local market a couple of miles from home starting at 5 AM on the weekends. I bicycled through some scary neighborhoods in our hometown of Windsor, Ontario, before sunrise in the darkness of early morning to get to that job. I was a determined young girl pedaling as fast as I could to avoid some of the crazy people I might encounter while on the way to work. I had some close calls, but thankfully I always managed to get there safely. I learned a lot from that experience. Keep your composure and just keep pedaling... FAST! I've taken that lesson to heart.

I worked all through high school and into university, where I had three jobs while always managing to keep my grades up. The oddest of the jobs I held was "grave digger." Yup! Some kids complain that they have to babysit to make spare change. I dug graves. It paid more than the other jobs and they needed people all the time, so there was always work. I even had to deal with some of the tasks involved in cremation. That was interesting. But I did it because I needed the money and it was honest work.

The willingness to work hard and serve others started really early in life for me. While both my parents' heritage is the same, their families could not be more different. My mom's family is Northern Italian. They walk the straight and narrow, are very serious and disciplined, driven, focused, and, like the weather up north, cooler in temperament. Northern Italians tend not to be super squishy or sentimental. They are practical and proud. My mom is a Leo (horoscope sign) and very much a lioness of her pride. She means business and isn't going to play. She believes in checks and balances and fairness for all. Growing up, she worked a lot. She exuded pride and strength. She is still that way. My mom was always very generous (I definitely got that from her and my maternal grandmother), and she was always extremely hardworking. In fact, I learned to serve and to be super generous with my time and efforts, almost to a fault, from her.

My dad's family was from Southern Italy. Southern Italians are very different from their neighbors to the north. They physically love hard (big kissers and huggers), and it's all about food, fun, and freedom. They live life with a no-regrets attitude and they are more carefree; often at whatever the cost! They tend not to place too much emphasis on the serious side of life. Our Nonni (grandparents) played a huge role in our life. All four of them really, but my dad's parents were directly involved with the daily care of raising my brother and me, especially after my parents' divorce. We ran to lunch there every day from school and then went there straight after school until I was deemed old enough to hang a key around my neck (a true latchkey kid) and go home on our own. They helped take care of my brother and me (plus our two cousins) while my mom worked, and they were very loving and caring to us. My grandfather was a walk-the-line kinda guy when it came to disciplining us. My Nonna is different. She ran around trying to make everyone happy. She would make sure we were all fed, and then she would head out to her second job, cleaning office buildings from 4 PM till midnight. Sometimes, if my grandpa wasn't yet home to care for us, we would have to go with her on the bus and tag along as she worked. We hid under the desks in the offices so she wouldn't get fired. "SHHHH!" she would say. "The big boss is here!" Lots of great memories were made. Sometimes, I miss those days.

My parents married young. They were high school sweethearts, and in reality, were just too different in their personalities, temperaments, and beliefs to make it as a happy couple. Dad was a crazy, live your life on the edge kinda guy, while mom was a calculated, straight, organized, much more disciplined, mature for her age, kinda gal.

When I was young, my parents owned a hardware store, and then purchased a second one with another family. Unfortunately, both families lost everything during the recession. My dad left, the businesses had failed, and this situation meant my mother became a single mom. This was never what she wanted. To this day, it has been the hardest hurdle for her to overcome. I don't think my dad realized the impact that would have on our family. Mom had at least two, often three, jobs and worked from 7 AM to 10 PM on weekdays and on weekends. This left me to watch over my brother, who is 15 months younger. I cooked, helped keep the house clean, made sure he got his schoolwork done and ate something—pretty much a blueprint for my future with my own family. I only have one sibling, and he means the world to me. It was us against the world... and the odds, for a lot of years!

I don't regret those times at all, or feel put upon. I was taught the value of work and responsibility from an early age. If you wanted something, you worked hard for it. I knew my mother was working as hard as she was so that my brother and I would be successful. She sacrificed a ton of her life for us, and for that, we're eternally grateful. Getting us to the finish line was her true life's goal, and we knew she loved us. Doing our part to make the household run more smoothly was just expected.

I know that I got this insane work ethic from my parents and grandparents, who, despite their differences, were all really, really hard workers. Both of my grandfathers were prisoners of war in Germany. They survived that horror and moved to Canada, looking for a better life. My maternal grandfather became a barber. He had a good trade and, with his work ethic, succeeded fairly quickly here in his new home country. Canada offered opportunities for advancement to immigrants. He eventually bought the building where his shop was (my maternal grandmother had the business sense and managed the finances and goings on of the business side) and then, later, the rest of the block. They built financial security, but not enough for ongoing generational wealth.

My paternal grandfather worked physically hard. He was a tomato harvester, then got into the roofing and siding trade. He worked long, hot days in the sun. He was physically exhausted when getting home. I remember him walking through the gate to his chair at the table, taking off his hat, and drinking that big highball icy drink my nonna prepared before he arrived home every day. My grandpa sponsored all of his brothers and sisters, and my grandmother's family as well, to come to Canada. He was the ONE to change the trajectory of their family's legacy and history. My maternal grandma, as I mentioned, cleaned offices at night for as long as I can remember. At one point, the whole family, numerous brothers and sisters and all the kids, lived in one small rumrunner house, taking turns at dinner and rotating meal times to get everyone fed. For the most part, they were all laborers, and they'd catch the bus out to the farms together. They also worked hard, but they had a different mindset about life. They were more relaxed in general with the idea that somehow, things would always work themselves out.

From mom, I learned discipline, focus, generosity, tough love, and intention. Mom taught me that to make a plan work, you had to see it through and stick with it. She believed that you worked hard and took pride in whatever you did. My mom was always early, ready, and super organized.

From dad, I got the creativity, the entrepreneurial spirit, the crazy, the survival instinct, the hunger, the quest for always wanting more, and the burning desire to live a life no one else was living! When an opportunity arose, it was my dad's spirit of adventure and risk-taking ability that carried me through the fear of potential failure. Failure is not an option! Failure is only failure if you give up or you quit!

These lessons from my parents and their parents continue to carry me and drive me forward. I'm passing them on to my children. And now, I'm sharing them with you.

As a self-made businesswoman, I've wanted to write this book for some time, mostly, admittedly, for other kick-ass business women (and their admirers too!), who are currently building their empires, and those who are dreaming of building their brand in the near future. Maybe you are doing all the supposedly right things, but you're not yet living the dream or seeing the return on life that you deserve. Maybe you don't know why you are working so hard and not achieving the freedom you've been dreaming about, but you have your eye on the prize and you aren't willing to give up!

Where is the financial freedom, the time freedom, and the life freedom that should be happening for you? Where will you be in five years, ten, and in retirement? Is there a plan to get to a place where you can just breathe? What does that even look like? What are you getting back from all you're giving? Do you even know what you want to get back? Can you define what freedom looks like for you?

Does this sound a little bit like you or someone you know?

In *The Multi-Million Dollar Mompreneur*, I'm going to tell you some of my stories and experiences—where I came from and how I got started—and to teach you some of the thoughtful and scrappy steps I took to get to where I am today. But this is not a self-aggrandizing memoir. I want to affect change. I want to create abundance for other people—including you. In the past, most of my own abundance came from adversity. At this point in my life, I am fortunate enough to be able to create abundance for others as well from generosity. I'm happy to share what I've learned to help you create abundance while avoiding all the pitfalls. Generosity truly breeds abundance!

> *Women just find a way to get it all done. We just figure it out. There's not really an option!*

I've distilled it all into 14 takeaways. Here's a preview of what's ahead:

- Why the first step in the journey to success is having a clear end destination
- How to take calculated risks and unleash the power of hardships
- Why it pays to forget about work/life balance and instead focus on harmony
- How to increase your quality of life along with your wealth
- Ways to make the most of credit and pay less (legally) in taxes
- How to teach your kids about money and get your whole family working together on building your business... and much more!

In the pages ahead, you'll also find action items–specific things you can do that will move you forward. I stepped on a lot of land mines along the way and made many mistakes, but I also made some very smart moves, found some systems that work, and used the lessons of my adversity to build wealth, both financially and personally. I want this book to help YOU avoid the pitfalls and glide over the hurdles much more easily than I did, and to take some of the steps I know would help by avoiding the costly mistakes! I want to compress the timeline to success while helping you quickly understand the things I've paid many mentors a lot of money over the years to figure out!

I understand busy professionals, business owners, entrepreneurs, and especially professional moms. Working women have so much going on. I know—I am one. I have four kids, all still in school. My work doesn't end when I kick off my high heels (or sneakers) at the end of the day.

While I hope men read this book (and I believe they will get a lot out of it), I wrote this book with women in mind. I love my family. I love being of service to them, to my clients, and even to my friends. It's just a fact that I am like most women. I wear a lot of hats, and sometimes it gets overwhelming. It's been my experience that women just find a way to get it all done. We just figure it out. There's not really an option!

Part of my daily routine, of course, includes work tasks, but my day doesn't end until the house is clean, the laundry is done, the family has been fed, and everyone has everything they need to be successful in school, work, and life. I am a full-time business owner, employer, wife, and mother. Oh, and as you'll learn throughout this book, my husband, Beau, is incredible. He's truly my biggest supporter and fan. Without his love, dedication and commitment to our dreams together, we would definitely not be able to do what we do. A supportive partner is one of the top indicators of success.

If any of this sounds like you, in any way, and you have a strong desire to make changes that will bring more abundance and the freedoms you want in your life, let's get to work! You really can have whatever you want. Your dreams can be your reality. You just have to decide that they will be.

ACTION ITEMS:

Think about your family and where you come from. How do their experiences and outlooks shape who you are today, especially when it comes to work, money, and success?

- ☐ What traits did you pick up from mom, dad, grandparents, or some caregiver?

- ☐ Do these traits propel you toward your dreams and goals, or do they get in the way of your success?

- ☐ Think of the things that add to your success. Write them down. Think of the things that may interfere with or inhibit your success. Write those down. Then compare your lists. Are there any surprises?

- ☐ What specific ideas or approaches to work and success are different from those things you were raised with or taught?

- ☐ What beliefs and generational characteristics are you passing on to your own children? Would you like to make any changes?

CHAPTER 1

START WITH THE END IN MIND, AND BELIEVE YOU'RE WORTH IT

I'm a firm believer in starting with the end in mind. Where are you now? Where do you want to go? Once we know that, we can figure the rest out.

I'm also a firm believer in recognizing your own worth, and that directly applies to success and money. How we think about money is intricately and intrinsically tied to how we think about our lives. Our mindset about money is a reflection of what we value, including ourselves. It's tied to our own self-worth.

Growing up in our household, no one ever talked about investing money, especially not in anything that could be construed as risky. You worked, you paid your bills, and what was left over went into the savings account. You saved as much as possible for that murky, scary, place where no one would be there to take care of you... ***the future***.

My grandpa owned his own business (a barbershop) and the apartment buildings above it. He knew he had to invest in himself and his business to grow, but even he took no real "**risky**" chances. In fact, my entire family bought into the view that money was somehow finite. They had the scarcity mindset. Their fears about money are understandable. They came from the perspective of having gone through the Great Depression and World War II, when money and common commodities were actually scarce. They held the belief that you had to save money as if no more could be made, no more would come. Once it was gone, it was gone, so you must save every penny possible. They were filled with doom and gloom, thinking that the bad times were always on the horizon. That rainy day was surely coming, so you had to prepare yourself for the worst possible scenarios.

My Nonna is 93 years old. There are things in her house from the 1920s. She saves everything, from leftovers to tin foil, and even reuses Ziplock bags. I get it. She lived through some seriously hard times when everything was scarce. My grandmother was born in 1931, and though they lived on a farm, there were a lot of siblings, I mean a whole lot, something like teens of them. They had no food other than what they could grow. She told me that there were times when she literally had to eat dirt because it contained much needed nutrients. I get why she saves stuff. From that perspective, we have never had that kind of lack. They lacked basic needs, so wealth wasn't even on their radar.

I did know that I was blessed with ability. I have a nearly photographic memory. I would sometimes be accused of cheating on a test because it was hard to believe that I could simply close my eyes and see the words on the pages of the textbooks floating in front of me. It's my superpower, and it makes me a really great visual learner. I am also A.D.H.D. (self-diagnosed), which, believe it or not, I don't see as a deficit or disorder or even a challenge. I see it as a genius trait, "an outlier" genetic anomaly, that works really, really, well for me. It makes me super hyper-focused on my goals. It pushes me toward a constant energy and mentality of abundance. I always had some form of self-worth, and I knew I had a gift. I believed in myself. If you don't believe in yourself, nobody will, and it's nearly impossible to truly succeed.

I knew I was a hard worker, a good student, and an intelligent person. Like many people, I believe we are never really good enough, but we strive to be better than we are today, even if it's just 1 percent better than we were yesterday. We can always do better, achieve more. This can be hard sometimes, but that mentality resulted in my pushing myself... always, always to do more, make more, excel in everything possible. I was the first person in my neighborhood and, in fact, in my family to get an education beyond high school. I wasn't even that sold on higher education. I just knew I needed to do something to help me level up. I took out student loans and worked many jobs at once to change my life.

I was NOT an overnight success! But I knew I wanted to succeed—I wanted to build my own business and achieve financial freedom. That was my end goal, and I kept working toward it.

The best way to create success is to commit to it. To be successful is to commit to your goals. This is a big thing for us. We are literally obsessed with our success and our goals. If you want to make your dreams come true, you have to become obsessed with your goals.

> *First, you need direction and purpose. You need a NORTH STAR.*

A clear vision of your goal is essential to your success. You need to define your goals and work backwards from that ideal to create a strategy that leads to your overall desired outcome.

First, you need direction and purpose. You need a NORTH STAR.

Second, you need to measure your success by establishing measurable goals or a benchmark.

Third, you need to decide the level of risk you're willing to take to get and stay there.

There are serious practical benefits to this method, both financially and psychologically. Knowing you have a well thought out plan keeps you committed to your mission, vision, and values and gives you the confidence that you will need to forge ahead when things come up to shake you.

CASE STUDY

If you want to buy a house or want to start a business or want to pay off debt, how much do you need? Start with the end in mind. Okay, you want to buy a $300,000 home; you need 20 percent down. That means you need a purpose, a clearly defined goal and a system of checks and balances of risk to get there. How much can you put away to get to this figure? How long will it take based on your salary, income or savings plan? A day, a week, a month? What are you going to use to get there? Will you set a certain amount of savings from your paycheck or income to raise the money you need for your down payment for training and marketing your new business? Do you need to create another stream of income, a side hustle? How are you going to create a side hustle that generates the amount you need? If you're living off all your income and need that extra money, saving is the unlikely path. Creating other streams of revenue may be the way to go.

You have to believe in yourself. You can't blame anyone else for your lack of success or your failures. We all make choices. No one told me to have four kids and run ten schools. Beau was thinking two kids, but he acquiesced (lol). You set priorities. They're your choices. Your goals and how you achieve them are your choices too.

My goal, even before I really knew what it meant, was that I was committed to being "the one"—the person who changed the trajectory of my family's life. As my nonno used to say, "it's not where you've been, but rather where you're headed that matters. It is not who you were, but who you will become." I've never dwelled or focused on my past. That causes stagnation, something I don't have time for. I've got too much to get done. I have always spent my energy in the present and in the future. One of my top five strengths (according to Gallup's Clifton Strengths Assessment, which you can take online for free) is futuristic. I have a natural inclination and ability to see what the future might hold. Like most women entrepreneurs, I am extremely visionary. I love to create.

I have friends who ask me, "Julie, when do you think enough will be enough? Why do you keep working, especially at the level you do?"

My answer is, "I don't know. I don't know why I keep working or why I do so much, but I truly love it!" It fuels me at every level of my existence.

My best guess is a few things are at play. Maybe it's the old scarcity mentality somewhere in that subconscious mind of mine, or that I honestly believe wholeheartedly that I still have so much to offer. In the back of my mind, maybe those niggling worms in my brain say, *all of this could end, all of this could be gone someday.* Maybe my grandmother's experiences are part of my DNA, or maybe the concept of doomsday stuck with me more than I might like to admit. Whatever the reason, I am not ready to say, "That's it, I've done enough." In some insane way, this fuels me. It pushes me to be more than just enough. I really feel like this next half of my life will be dedicated to helping others succeed. Generosity breeds abundance.

I didn't allow my personal or financial mindset to be one of scarcity. As I grew older and had many experiences, lots of education, and traveled as much as I could, I learned and expanded my mindset of growth. Hard work didn't scare me. My parents gave me that, and I knew that if I wanted something, I could work for it and work toward it and never quit till I realized that objective. Convince yourself first. No dream felt too big. The only issue is that our goals are generally not big enough.

When I got into college, I eventually thought I might become a lawyer. Super safe, right? Lawyers make big bucks, right? They drive nice cars; they have nice houses. Someone will always need to hire a lawyer, so there will always be work, right?

During my second and third year of college, I went to Europe to play soccer, have fun, study, experience European culture, and as they used to say, "find myself." I spent a lot of time in France and when I came back, I was out of funds and needed to move back in with my mother while I regrouped.

By that time, I realized I didn't want to be a lawyer any longer. I discovered, sort of by accident, that I loved Montessori and teaching. This realization came about because I needed a job. I met a woman who was running a private Montessori school out of our local high school. She needed help, and the work appealed to me. She hired me to assist with the early morning and after-school program, among other tasks that would free her up to run her business, but before long, I was doing more and more. Soon, I was the one running nearly all aspects of her business, and I LOVED IT!

Beau and I had been dating on and off since our college days. Now that I was back home, we reconnected. "If we're going for a drink, we're getting married," was his blunt but realistic statement. Obviously, he was right. We went out for a drink and set a date, and we've been married with four kiddos for over 20 years now.

So, here I was, living with my mother, and determined to make a future for myself. I knew I wanted to start a school, and I asked her if I could use her basement to start a Montessori summer preschool. I set up a pseudo classroom with some supplies I bought from Walmart and the dollar store, making lots of my own teaching supplies. Before long, I had 11 students, ages four to six mostly. The first summer showed proof of concept in my Montessori school, but my mom was like, "You're not doing this in my basement forever."

I needed capital to grow and take this idea out of my mom's house. Initially, the goal was to start a preschool serving kids, ages two-and-a-half to six. (In Canada, kids can start elementary school as young as three years and eight months old, and public education is decent.) There was a church that agreed to rent me their basement to run a school during the day. But I would need rent money, rezoning, approvals from the city, and some money to get all the essentials to make the school viable. We would have to build shelves and cubbies. We needed tables and chairs.

Along with Beau, my grandpa, my stepdad, my dad, my brother, and Beau's dad volunteered to help me do the building stuff. Grandpa would also continually help with the landscaping. My dad knew how to help with the zoning and building. My mom ended up working with us and, as we grew, she was soon running the whole accounting department of our portfolio of schools. It was a family affair.

You will see me repeat the idea of "starting with the end in mind" a lot in this book. Bear in mind that the end can sometimes be the end of one phase that leads to the next and the next. I calculated exactly how much I would need to get my school together in that church basement. I determined that $25,000 would do it.

I had the drive, the will, and free labor, but where would I get the money? I did not want to borrow from friends and family. I wanted to show them I could do this on my own. My stubborn independence has, in most cases, served me extremely well.

ACTION ITEMS:

Think about your end goal, your ultimate vision for success. Then, think about the steps you need to take to get there—starting TODAY.

- ☐ What is your end goal? Write it down and make it as specific and concrete as possible.

- ☐ How are you going to get there? What resources do you need?

- ☐ Who are the people you need to help you get there?

- ☐ What is the noise you must erase around you?

- ☐ What are you doing today to help you get closer to that goal?

CHAPTER 2

EMBRACE ADVERSITY TO CREATE ABUNDANCE

As luck would have it, I was perusing the local paper and saw an ad.

Borrow $25,000, no credit check, no problem! The ad had no phone number to call, and there was no emailing people at that time in history. All it said was to apply; come in person to this address.

So, I went, with Beau by my side. The address was in a downtown location, which was on the seedy side. You only went downtown at night to enjoy the nightlife and got out fast, but not during the day to hang out.

The address advertised led us to a back alley and a maroon exterior hallway door behind McDonald's, with the number from the ad posted on it. No sign, no business name, just a door. This was not some nightmare I had or something from a scary movie. This was the real thing.

"Should we do this?" Beau asked.

"We're here. Let's see what the deal is." I answered.

Beau pulled the door handle, and we entered a small, very plain room. There were two folding chairs, nothing on the walls, and a rickety table, behind which sat one tall skinny dude. He didn't smile once.

"You here about the loan?" he asked gruffly.

"Yes, we are. I guess we're in the right place," I replied.

"Yup!"

He proceeded to explain "the deal." He introduced himself as Malcolm Bhanks, no pun intended, and told us that the loan would be for $25,000 at a 19 percent per diem. So yeah, he was a loan shark. Without mincing words, he said that we would have one year to pay the loan back in full, and if we missed payments or failed to complete the transaction, Beau would basically be a goner. Visions of Beau in cement shoes by the river flashed in my mind. It was a high interest loan with death as the collateral.

You know a man loves you when he hears these terms and signs the papers with you, anyway. Which he did. That one action changed the course of our lives. Behind that door—fear—got us to where we are today. If we had never crossed that threshold of fear, we would not be million-aires today. Never. No way.

To this day, we talk about scary Malcolm and the leap of faith that changed everything. We remember how the day we signed on that dotted line with a humorless loan shark affected the rest of our lives. The blessing? It was the adversity.

Yes, ADVERSITY creates ABUNDANCE.

Paying that loan back was NOT an option. Ask Beau! No cement shoes.

- FAILURE wasn't an option. I believed it in my mind. I saw it clearly, before I even signed that loan, that this was going to be all it turned out to be!
- I ENVISIONED what this would look like in the end. I manifested this in my head well before it came to fruition.
- Having motivation, willpower, and drive were not options. They were non-negotiables.
- Getting up each and every day despite the challenges was NOT an option! It was that or default on Malcolm's scary loan. I didn't once even think about the what ifs. The excitement of the dream and the goal was my ultimate fuel.

> "*Success was not an option. It was the ONLY option!! I became obsessed with my success!*

Failure is NOT an option. Don't fool yourself into believing it is. Learning from mistakes, growing, changing, and challenging yourself to do things better or differently is the alternative to failure.

Failure only happens when you quit. If you learned a lesson and didn't quit, you didn't fail.

Success was not an option. It was the ONLY option!! I became obsessed with my success!

Most of my life, my family felt the need to constantly remind me of their beliefs about money with words like, "Well, you know, the way that you spend, you won't have any left for troubled times. You do realize that doomsday is coming. How will you make it?" Spending money was under the microscope of scrutiny in every situation. I would answer with, "I don't know what I'm going to do. Maybe what everyone else does when it happens?" I figured if something cataclysmic like another world war or depression or, I don't know, a global pandemic happened, we would all be in the same boat. So, that happened, and here we are on the other side of it. Your money mindset is a deep part of who you were and where you came from, so you need to change it to be who you wish to become!

My family's perspective was about more than a money mindset; it was about their wealth mindset. Wealth only happened through saving. If you saved every penny possible, by the time you reached old age, you would have some version of wealth. The idea that you could invest money, aka take a chance on something and spend money in an effort to exponentially increase your wealth, was unthinkable. They didn't think about wealth. They thought about income. This seemed counterintuitive to me. How much could I possibly save and how long would it take to be "wealthy?" In fact, how much money makes you "wealthy?" What if my savings outlived me?

> *Your money mindset is a deep part of who you were and where you came from, so you need to change it to be who you wish to become!*

I didn't grow up in scarcity in terms of food and shelter (our basic needs were generally met), but there were moments when I felt some emotional scarcity. Wealth is not only about money.

So, how is money mindset a reflection of personal mindset? We need money in this world to make the things we want to happen, well, happen. It's a fact. If we believe that money will be scarce, it stems from a lack of belief in abundance in our personal life. We can always make money. Money is readily available. If we believe we have value, we will know that we deserve to be successful, both financially and personally.

Going for your dreams might be scary, and I am not at all suggesting you borrow money from a loan shark. But if you don't have a rich parent or long lost aunt who left you a big inheritance, you have to take a chance on your BHAG—Big Hairy Audacious Goal—and find a way to make it happen. Your big goal, your dream, will not only affect your life but more than likely, it will affect a lot of other people's lives. Most of us have dreams that are bigger than ourselves. You must commit, stay the course, and see it to fruition. Success is your duty—for yourself, for your kids, and for your family.

I knew I could run a successful school. I knew what it took, and more importantly, I believed that whatever I didn't know, whatever skills I lacked, I could learn. I could figure it out. Pure fire and the will to succeed were greater than any fear I had about signing that loan.

I started that Montessori preschool in the basement of St. Paul's church with 13 kids. A few came along from my original makeshift summer school in my mom's basement. I had a huge desire to create an exceptional Montessori preschool environment for all children. I wanted to impact 1000 families. My WHY was so much bigger than me. I listened to no one. I blocked out all the noise. I shushed the naysayers. Trust me, there were lots of negative Nellies telling me I couldn't do it! I was hyper-focused on my goals and dreams and on paying back that loan. I let the naysayers talk, they had nothing on me. I calculated every detail—rent, $1500 a month; pay Malcolm's loan first, roughly $1200 (the church would not break anyone's legs if we were a few days late); buy supplies, which came to roughly $5000 a month, adding in food and all the things I needed to run the school and not get killed by Malcom; and market it. I did the math on how many students I would need to reach the results I was aiming for. I diligently worked backwards, getting through each month a little more out of the red. After I got to that end result... well, we'll get to what happened after I hit that goal in a bit.

My mindset has always been really strong even in the worst of times. This reflected in my money mindset. I went right to figuring out solutions. I am a solution-based thinker! I had my priorities in the right place, and I had a "survival instinct" and an insane drive like no other. Beau's life was never really on the line. The one thing adversity in life brings us is an overwhelming and powerful will to succeed. You don't just want it—you need it like the air you breathe. You dig deep and you pull out your all. The one thing our old hood taught us was that we were survivors. That inner fire, killer instinct, and drive is not something you can buy, but it is something that sets us apart. It runs deep.

I organically grew that preschool into one with 75 students in our first year. And, we paid Malcolm back in one year! Sure, we got creative at times. Without the staff knowing the behind-the-scenes 'drama,' we paid them with Beau's paychecks when we had to, and we did lots of shuffling (lots of transfers to and from various bank accounts and lines) to make things work. There were many Fridays when Beau ran to the bank to put his check in just in time to cover payroll until tuition money came in. No matter what, we figured it out.

I was the teacher, accountant, enrollment gal, chef, and janitor. We even had to build all the components of the classroom on wheels because we had to tear down the whole room at the end of every day by 6 pm so the church could use the basement for evening events. We had to roll up the carpets, mop the floor, clean up the kitchen, put everything in the space they designated to us in the storage room, and fully clean the rooms before we left. Every morning, we came in an hour early to pull it all out again and reset the entire school up. Now, that's what you call dedication. Beau would come home from work—he was working full time at a hospital and in the middle of his dissertation—and go directly to the preschool to meet me and help me mop, clean, and prep for the next day. We did that for two years. His commitment to me and this crazy dream never wavered. I brought in my cousin Dana to help, poor girl (I often ran her ragged). She had worked with me in the preschool at the high school, and I asked her if she wanted to come work for me full time. We ran the day-to-day operations, just the two of us. She helped me a ton. I owe her a world of thanks! We owe so many people so much thanks!

Yes, I am lucky that I had the support of a really incredible life partner and the support of our family. You may or may not have that, but you have yourself—and that's a lot. Our parents helped us so much, too. They later gave us the opportunity for creative financing using credit lines to expand, but even those were paid back quickly. If there is a WILL, there is always a way. You have to look for it, get creative, and not be afraid to ask for help.

Adversity breeds abundance. There's a special something that adversity teaches you that nothing else can. I'm going to share many more stories of adversity that we lived through… Some were worse than others. The main thing to realize is that your dreams can be your reality. But first, you have to change your mindset so you can live the life you deserve, a life you really, truly love.

I have a strong mentality around failure. I share this with my kids. When is enough, enough? How much do you put in? How I feel about failure is that you only fail if you quit. If you learn a lesson, it's not a failure. My failure mentality was developed as a young child. I heard a lot of interesting things from people growing up, which I later had to reframe for myself.

You don't take risks because failure is looming behind you. You don't attempt things because you're afraid. Sound familiar? If you don't reframe this for yourself, you lose out on so many opportunities. On the other side of fear is a whole new life for yourself. If you can push through to the other side of fear, it's where you find your true, new self. Fear is an inhibiting factor. We are told, "Don't climb that tree. You could fall." "Don't try that. It's too dangerous." "Don't quit that job you hate. You will never find one better." There is not a risk-taking mentality taught to most people. Instead, our parents, school, teachers, lots of people share all their warning labels that they put on nearly everything. We spend the greater part of our days in public school being taught how to be sheep, not shepherds. The shepherds like us don't fit the mold of what the government needs from society... they need workers, not more leaders!

It seems as if most of us are afraid to let our kids take risks. We become helicopter parents who inhibit our kids' growth. My husband, Beau, is not having that. He is all about pushing the kids into adversity. He believes that adversity is the way they learn. We are creating a mentality of "adversity breeds abundance" with our children. He believes adversity breeds excellent character and that it also breeds abundance. It's taken me a bit, but I'd have to agree it has been life-altering for all of them. My son was very depressed when we moved to Omaha, Nebraska. He left a small school in Windsor, Ontario, where he was a big fish to come into a huge school where he literally knew no one. He missed his friends. He was so unhappy, and the school system and people were really very different. I was upset and crying about this all the time. I hated to see my son so unhappy. Beau's answer was, "Someday this will serve him well."

"I don't see how," was my response. How that could be right. I was Mom, crying my eyes out. I just wanted to soothe my son and make things better for him.

Years later, when my son went to college, he said, "Mom, thank you for pushing us to move here. I hated you guys so much for doing this, but I was much better prepared for college and life than I would've ever been if we stayed in Windsor. There's so much more opportunity here. I am so grateful." So, oh my God! Beau was right. That happens more often than not.

The other side of fear is where you find your courageous self. If you don't get there, you remain living in the shadows of doubt, shame, guilt, and despair. For a lot of people, success is limited, or at least defined by their acceptance or denial of fear.

ACTION ITEMS:

Think about your money mindset and attitude toward adversity:

- ☐ Did you grow up with an abundance or scarcity mindset? Has that changed?

- ☐ What money mindset "traumas" have you gone through?

- ☐ How are you working on building an abundant mindset?

- ☐ What would you risk to achieve a dream goal?

- ☐ Are you in circles with people who lift you up and move you forward, or are you in circles with folks who are pulling you down?

- ☐ How can you solve someone else's problem? As that is the true reason for any business.

- ☐ Do you let your kiddos go out there and face adversity, or are you a protective parent who wants to scoop them up and protect them from overcoming life's challenges?

CHAPTER 3

HARMONIZE YOUR WORK AND FAMILY

E veryone talks about striving for work/life balance. In this chapter, I want to reveal one of my biggest secrets—one that kept me going as a mom, a wife, and an entrepreneur. Balance is baloney. Instead, I embrace work/life HARMONY.

The most successful movie ever for Warner Bros. helps to back up my truth. Have you seen the *Barbie* movie? The monologue beautifully delivered in the film by America Ferrara really hit home. She sums it up perfectly in less than two minutes.

Here is a taste of what she says:

> *"It is literally impossible to be a woman. You are so beautiful, and so smart, and it kills me that you don't think you're good enough. Like, we have to always be extraordinary, but somehow, we're always doing it wrong...*

> *"... I'm just so tired of watching myself and every single other woman tie herself into knots so that people will like us. And if all of that is also true for a doll just representing women, then I don't even know."*
>
> Watch the movie and listen to the rest of this monologue. She hits home with all of it.

Parenthood is just hard. It is the absolute most rewarding and the most difficult thing I have ever had to do. Being a multi-million dollar mama is another level of hard. It is a matter of choosing which hard things you're going to tackle, day by day, moment by moment.

Balancing a professional career or being an entrepreneur while raising your children is something many folks, especially women, find difficult to talk about. Having an incredible partner to do this with has been a lifesaver. I realize that not everyone has an incredible partner or the support of their family the way I do. There are so many expectations placed on us as women in general that adding the titles of entrepreneur and business professional just lengthens the list and ramps up the pressures.

The journey that professional women trapeze through is literally insane. We are expected to be and do everything, and we convince ourselves that we should be able to do everything, that we can do everything, and then we do everything... and then some.

So, where do I start to explain how I approached my work and my family, how I first became a "million-dollar mama" and what that took to make millions? I guess at the beginning might be best. I had my first baby, Xavier, and the day after he was born, I was at the office stitched up to God knows where. I couldn't even sit but stood there doing payroll with him next to me in his carrier on the floor by my desk. I refused any and all pain meds so I could focus on the work I had to catch up on. The next day, I returned to work in full-force mode, breastfeeding and pumping in between work breaks, with a baby that wouldn't latch and "poison milk" (as my nonna called it). She honestly believed that Xavier was full-blown colic due to the stress I was under and that somehow that stress made its way to my milk (Welcome to all things superstition when you're Italian). Regardless, I returned to work like nothing had just happened. Childbirth? Meh, no worries.

I had a couple more kids and added a few more schools with each pregnancy. There was an ongoing joke that whenever I got pregnant, a new school was around the corner. Funny thing was they were right. We were in super high growth mode, adding both kids and schools at a colossal pace. During my last pregnancy, I vividly remember puking under my desk in a wastebasket through what felt like an absolute eternity of my pregnancy with Xoë. I've schlepped kids with me to work since the day after their births (what maternity leave?!!) and breastfed till breakdowns when my milk wouldn't come while being told to "relax " as I was running a multi-million dollar empire!

The worst part of this story is that it's probably not unfamiliar to most of you reading this book. If you're a man reading this book, you can take it all in too, or just fully skip this chapter, but the harsh truth is y'all should really pay the most attention here!

People always talk about balance. One of the most remarkable aspects of this multi-million dollar mama's journey is the belief in my ability to HARMONIZE the demands of motherhood and the famous "invisible" load along with my professional pursuits.

I gotta ask... **WHAT BALANCE?** There's a continual push-pull of expectations. Be a great mom, a great wife, a kick-ass entrepreneur, a caretaker for your parents and grandparents, a good sibling, a great aunt, a phenomenal leader, and the list goes on... all placed on me by society and mainly set by **yours truly**. Truth is, there's no one to blame but good ol' me. The idea of consistently having to choose between my children and my work has been an ongoing struggle for years. There is no balance. At best, sometimes, we have harmony.

Sure, I missed out on a lot; lots of sporting events, concerts, school interviews etc. I was also probably judged for this by those with some sharp tongues and loose lips and reminded of that by family and friends a few times (both to my face and behind it). But I continued on, ignoring the naysayers, knowing that the final goal would be so sweet and incomprehensible to most of them. I was doing what most **would not**, so I could eventually live like most **could not**. We were/are extremely blessed that we had a very supportive family. My grandparents babysat the kids every day until they were ready to attend the preschools full-time. I truly think it filled their buckets as much or more than it filled ours. Our parents and family helped us out so much with the running of the schools (accounting, grocery shopping, fixing/maintaining things, watching kids for date nights, conferences, and the like). We hired a nanny when Xander was born. She was a true blessing to our family, and remained with us for 14 years. She passed away last year from cancer, and we were all equally devastated. I wouldn't have been able to run an empire without all of the help from the people mentioned above. Everyone played an integral part in our success. It was a true family affair.

Nothing came easy. I guess I wanted to write this chapter to reiterate this. For many multi-million dollar mamas, the path to financial success involves creating their own businesses from the ground up or investing strategically. The road to financial success as a mother is not without its obstacles. From societal expectations to personal doubts, multi-million dollar mamas encounter numerous challenges along the way. I had to overcome many of these hurdles by sheer determination and by committing to and being obsessed with our success.

The idea of "mompreneurship" has taken on a whole new meaning. It represents a powerful group of women who are successfully **harmonizing** the challenges of childrearing with the demands of building their own business empires. It is not a balance, nor an easy feat!

Start by identifying your non-negotiables. What do you refuse to compromise on? What matters most to you? What time and energy can you spend on work or family or yourself, and NOT feel guilty about it? Guilt is the absolute worst—it's debilitating. Mammas, we are really bad at this. Then, create specific goals for yourself, your business, and your family. These goals should be measurable, and time bound. Our business goal was to impact 1000 children per year. (Yay! We did it!) Our family goal was to get to all of the seven continents together. Finally, we accomplished that in December 2023, by braving the insane seas and wild and surreal terrain of Antarctica! And lastly, my personal goal was to become an expert in my field and to help others rise alongside us (Well, here I am, working hard to help as many folks as I can).

Becoming a million, then a multi-million dollar mama is a remarkable achievement that deserves celebration. It's an inspiring testament to the limitless potential of hard working mothers. It's a journey marked by passion, dedication, and the unshakable belief that being a mom and achieving financial success are not mutually exclusive. Women entrepreneurs with children serve as role models, proving that with the right mindset and determination, any mother can rewrite her story and become a multi-million dollar mama.

I get asked a lot about how I "harmonized" work and raising a family, so wanted to share some tips on what helped me (as a super control freak, high ADHD/OCD entrepreneur and mama) get through:

Developing effective time management strategies. For me, time blocking and my calendar saved me. Use your color coded calendar and time block all the kids' activities you need/want to get to. Time block your personal time (at least a couple of interrupted hours a week), and finally, time block all of your work commitments. BE REALISTIC. Do what works for you.

Finding people who can help you get things done. Understand you can't do everything on your own. Outsource any non-essential tasks. Grab online groceries, hire a laundry company, grab a VA to do your graphics, outsource more meticulous work tasks to a third party company like

Upwork or Fiverr. At home, involve everyone in the household chores and set expectations. And don't be afraid to reach out to family and friends for help. We all need a village!

Being open and honest. Talk to your partner, your family, your colleagues, and friends about your priorities and the challenges you are facing in balancing all of your roles effectively. Make sure everyone is on the same page and that they all understand your commitments. Someone has to pick up the slack when you can't. Who will that be?

Being flexible. You may need to change your priorities from time to time, and that is okay. Sometimes as moms, our kiddos need more attention (they're sick, they're having a bad day, they have an important school event we need to be at). Sometimes, it's your business that requires extra attention (opening a new location, you're in the middle of a raise, you're training new staff or onboarding C suite execs).

Learning to say NO. You can't do everything, so stop trying. It's not selfish; it's protecting your peace, your space, and it shows that you are committed to your worth. You must learn to say no to people, commitments, or opportunities that do not align with your priorities. If it isn't helping you get to your North Star, then you can't spend time or energy on it.

ACTION ITEMS:

☐ How well do you manage your time? Consider time blocking or another method to help you.

☐ Do you have a village you can rely on? If not, start reaching out and building one!

☐ Prioritize your health and well-being. You aren't good to anyone if you aren't healthy.

☐ Make time for self-care. Schedule those manis, pedis, and facials!

☐ Celebrate your successes as a mom and as an entrepreneur, both big and small!

CHAPTER 4

TEACH YOUR KIDS "BUSINESS AND LIFE 101"

I love to cook. My grandmother taught me all her tricks, how to make homemade pasta, ravioli, and gnocchi from scratch. I can still remember barely seeing over the kitchen table and rolling those gnocchi out one fork at a time! I'm a vegetarian, yet somehow, I am a killer cook when it comes to any Italian dish. My mom cooked a lot too. In fact, my sense of smell is my greatest sense and any smells of homemade salsa (tomato sauce) or Chicken Fettina (breaded fried cutlets) brings a sense of immediate euphoria (even though I don't eat meat). It feels like home! Funny thing, now my kids come home and the first thing they say is, "Mom, it smells sooo good in here!" (Chicken Fettina for the win!) I had that with both my mom and my grandmother, and I wanted my kids to have that same experience when they come home from college or a long day at school or sports. "I can smell the Fettina!" they'll say. My kids do things like put my chicken cutlets in Ziplock bags and stuff them in their pockets or backpacks on their way to practice or events. "Fast protein hit, Mom." They love my cooking, and I love that they do. It's a full circle kind of thing; part of my history will inevitably be part of theirs.

Yes, I can hire a cook and a cleaning person. I can do less work around the house. I do have someone who comes in twice a month and does a deep cleaning—that's for my sanity—but I love cooking for my family. I like a clean house (I'm definitely a bit OCD) and I want things organized and in the right space and place. I take great pride in my home and I love the smell and look of a good, clean house! How you do one thing is how you do... everything! The neighborhood kids always comment on our signature house scent. One even said. "Mrs. Roy, I was at Bath and Body Works yesterday, and it smelled like your house!!" I had to laugh. Sweet kiddos!

When it comes to raising our kids, Beau and I have learned to merge our parenting styles and mindsets. He comes from a very different kind of family unit. He is the oldest of three, the only boy, and, according to his folks, he was always a good kid, very active, kind and caring. He is more than a decade older than his youngest sister, so that gave him a perspective on raising daughters from watching his parents and having to be the big brother. His parents are calm, cool, and collected. They have been married since forever and have a great relationship. I'm not saying my husband grew up in some TV fantasy family, but he does see parenting a bit differently than I do. So, we compromise. We discuss. We blend our styles, and we pray we don't screw up (which is impossible, everyone makes mistakes). We wanted to create a unified approach on what we delivered to the kids. That's super important. It doesn't always work, and it's a consistent commitment. You must aim to be unified though or things start to fall apart. It is hard to be unified when you come from two very different worlds. We have had and continue to have long conversations about the end goal and how we want it to look.

For example, I still have the Italian guilt method of dealing with the kids at times. I can start a guilt trip over something with one of the kids and Beau will quickly point that out.

"You're doing it again!"

"I know, I know, but I am so good at it."

I would try to treat all the kids the same, but Beau would remind me that they are individuals, and we have to parent each of them as such.

Beau would say, "We can't treat them the same way."

I would disagree, "Yes, we can. Fair is fair."

"Okay, but fair is not equal." His response frustrated me at first, but mostly because he was right. So, I would have to learn to modify my parenting style. That wasn't comfortable, but I learned that the compromises made for better parenting and happier, healthier kids. I admit that Beau was the driving force behind our parenting paradigm. If you ask me, he is the better parent—and don't worry, he knows that (lol). He's so much like his dad, such a caring, nurturing, really good dad, no manipulation, just all the love coupled with a "be what you want to be" mindset. He is super supportive of our kids and of me, for that matter.

I can helicopter with all the kids, but especially with my daughter. Things are not as simple as when I was a kid.

Truth is, no one seemed to care where we neighborhood kids were until the street lights came on. Be home by dark, home for dinner, get your schoolwork done, and go to bed. If someone scraped a knee or got stung by a bee, they went to whoever's house was closest and someone tended to that. It's scarier today. I want to know where my kids are at all times. It feels like the world is a lot less safe, especially for young women.

I was the "one," the person in my family who broke the money mindset cycle. There has to be at least one person in the family to do that to change generational wealth. For many families, that never happens. They stay in whatever money position they were always in, generation to generation. They remain lower income, working class, middle income, even upper middle income families, generation to generation. No one breaks the mold. For generations, in America, trade jobs—like plumber, electrician, carpenter, or other hands-on work—became the family business in a sense. Father to son or daughter, kids went into the same field or occupation their parents did. Even teachers' kids many times become teachers. Work, save, buy a house, raise the family, rinse and repeat. That's the American dream. But is it really a dream worth pursuing?

When one person in the family changes the money mindset, that person changes the generational trajectory of the family and the future generations. I was that one. Now, Beau and I are on the path to make sure our children continue the road we have paved for ourselves, for them, and the generations to follow. We are seriously committed to our legacy, and we are intentional about doing all the things that are required to make that happen.

> *Work, save, buy a house, raise the family, rinse and repeat. The American dream... but is it really?*

For starters, we make use of the things we can do for them because we have the income to do it. We started a Custodial Roth IRA for each of them as soon as we were able to. It's possible to start a Custodial Roth IRA for your kids as early as their first birthday. If you can put in $6,500 a year, they will have roughly $200,000 by the time they are 18 and getting ready for college. We did this with our kids when they were little. They can't get into it or make use of it without us while they are underage.

Once our kids were of age to work, we began to make use of a way to give them money, get a tax break, and teach them how to use money in the best ways. We create an LLC for each of them. We chose a generic enough name for their "company," so that they can make use of it later in life. LLCs can do business under different names as DBAs—Doing Business As. So, under Roy Holdings Inc., we can have many DBAs.

You may not know this, but if you own a business, you can hire your kids and pay them for their meaningful work. They can be on payroll and make a wage in exchange for any work assigned, or they can be hired as models for your advertising. The work assigned to them must be legit. It might be pool cleaning, filing paperwork, babysitting the younger siblings, lots of things, and this money is a tax deduction for your business. If they are hired for advertising, you can pay them and claim it as a business expense if you create a family management company. Your CPA can do this for you. Make sure to ask your CPA and Lawyer to review all suggestions as I am neither- we speak only about our personal experiences in this book.

What we do with this money, greatly impacts how our kids work with money. We follow what is referred to as the 50/40/10 rule. 50 percent of the money must be put into savings—$6500 gets put into their Custodial Roth IRA. This is not negotiable. I know I have said that saving isn't everything, but it's not nothing either. We teach the kids that putting money into savings will have rewards down the line. We then have them flip these IRA's into real estate investments down the line.

The next 40 percent is theirs to spend. They can buy something they want with the money. They can save it for something bigger; what they choose to do with that money is all on them.

The final 10 percent must be used for something of a charitable nature, a social passion they have. We want them to understand gratitude at a deep level and to love contributing to the benefit of other people. For example, Xoë loves animals. She can use that final 10 percent of her money for animal shelters, such as the Humane Society—food and toys for animals in shelters. This is helpful to us as parents because we learn more about our kids this way. We get to see what is in their hearts, what their passions are, and what drives them. Having their own earned income teaches kids the real value of money.

THE DIFFERENCE BETWEEN AN IRA AND A ROTH IRA

IRA stands for Individual Retirement Account. A Roth IRA (named after Senator Willam Roth) is a bit different. For one thing, if the required conditions are met, it's generally not taxed upon distribution.

The main difference between Roth IRAs and most other IRAs is that qualified withdrawals from the Roth IRA are tax-free as well as growth in the account. Also, with a Roth IRA, you might have investments in stocks and bonds, securities, mutual funds and even real estate. Bottom line, there are less restrictions on the kinds of investments that can be made and more tax advantages.

We had specific goals with our kids. Worldly education was the most important thing. We knew we wanted to travel. We set a goal to take our kids to see all seven continents and we did it. We wanted them to have life experiences that allowed them to navigate the whole world, not just our corner of it. By seeing other countries, they learned about other cultures, and it has made them more inclusive, and more accepting of all kinds of people, not just the ones they grew up with. We believed in "classrooms without walls." They learned how other people think, live, and breathe. When you are more educated, you appreciate the world around you. My kids are super lovers of humans. They can talk to anybody from any walk of life and communicate and appreciate them.

The big thing was to create as supportive an environment as possible for them, but still make it clear we are striving for excellence and exceptionalism in all aspects of their growth. We try to enjoy every day as there are no guarantees. Excellence doesn't mean perfection or that you have to be great at everything. We want our kids to understand that if they are capable of excellence, they should achieve it. Put in as much as you can to provide excellence, whether it's for you or for others.

Then there is the fact of entrepreneurship. They grew up around it. They have always been in the position where they see us working, excelling, creating, and pushing to achieve another level. We want that for them because the best example is seeing us actually doing it. We included them in that as soon as they could be involved. I have pictures of them as youngsters opening boxes and flipping schools with us. Now they walk properties and look at pro-formas. We take them to many conferences so they can see what other people like us are doing, too. Exposure is key.

They do go to public school, which, I admit, typically creates sheep, not shepherds. I get it. That's how a society sustains itself. We need workers and public schools to help build that workforce. But we did not want to go the private school route with them. We wanted them in a multifaceted environment. Our public school isn't even diverse enough, truth be told. Obviously, they had our Montessori preschool education but once they were of school age, we sent them to the public schools in Canada and continued to do so once we moved to the States. We encourage them to save to invest.

They actually started in a French school in Canada. They are bilingual, and in fact, Beau's dad taught in a full French

School. Canada is super multi-cultural, very inclusive, and open, offering lots of opportunity. Everyone gets the same education, the same system, and there is not a big push for private schools there other than preschool. A Montessori preschool education gave our kids the foundation we believe in—problem-solving, leadership training, thinking outside the box, emergent learning, independence, multi-age classrooms with the older peers helping the younger peers creating that generosity, and all the things we wanted for them to get an exceptional head start in life.

When we moved to the States, the schools were very different. While all of our kids do very well academically, they had trouble fitting into the mold of American public schools. Being raised with an entrepreneurial spirit and mindset, our children think differently and act differently than most other kids, which can sometimes cause social issues for them. It wasn't always easy for them to make friends who understood where they were coming from. The rigidity of the school environments with no ability to think outside the box didn't sit well with them. In middle school and high school, public schools present information and material students are expected to digest, memorize, and regurgitate rather than allowing them to explore ideas and arrive at their own conclusions. They don't encourage critical thinking and discovery. They generally don't encourage solution-based thinking.

My second son, Xander, is very academic and thinks more linearly. He's left-brained, like Beau, who is a doctor. In a way, the public school system worked for him, but he also has my entrepreneurial mindset. He wants to be a doctor, a radiologist, so college is a must for him. He knows he wants to work a flexible schedule as a doctor, while creating a passive income stream through owning his own real estate (medical building), and he wants to have other doctors and medical professionals and labs rent space from him. He knows that if he doesn't want to work hard forever, diversifying his income streams and creating passive income is an absolute must. Xander appreciates that learning certain things was a waste of his time. We had to have lots of conversations with all of our kids about what to take forward into their future and what things might be set aside. We explained that even though some of the learning tasks might not be conducive to their future education or plans, learning a variety of subjects would make them more well-rounded humans.

My daughter, Xoë, is 12 (she's the youngest and only girl of the four kids). Xoë has the mindset of a 20-year-old. Her schoolmates, especially the girls, want to talk more about their crushes, celebrities, and social media influencers, whereas she is more concerned with social issues. She is not concerned with gossip, which boy is cute or who likes who. She wants to talk about life, current events, and some of the subject matter they are learning about. We may be dealing with this type of issue more than most parents, but that's because of the way we've raised our kids.

Xavier is very much the same. He is a freshman in college. We went to his commencement ceremony and the speaker's topic was, oddly enough, about how failure is an option. This is, of course, the exact opposite of what we have taught them their whole life. During the event, Xavier texted me to say, "Mom, what in God's name are we doing here?"

I was thinking those exact words.

Xavier continued to say, "Okay, so if failure is an option, why are these people in the caps and gowns being celebrated? They're the ones who didn't fail. The whole system is set up to pass a set of courses, to get the highest GPA. The whole entire school system is based on NOT failing."

Yup! I was thinking the exact same thing as he was putting it into words.

He told me about a college professor who was expounding on how debt was bad. "Don't allow yourself to get into debt," the prof warned them.

"Mom," Xavier said to me, "I appreciate the teacher, but in reality, he is making a modest salary compared to what you make and you have very different views on debt. There's good debt and bad debt. It's all about how you leverage it."

Xane, our third son, talks a lot about his future and his love of real estate and entrepreneurship. He is a friendly, sweet, smart, and very creative kiddo (very right-brained). He has a love for history, people, relationships, and life. He has the gift of communication. He can communicate so well with anyone about anything. Warren Buffet has said there's one skill to get in life: the ability to communicate. I think Xane is set, Warren!

If I may say so myself, "YES! We're teaching them the right mindset." Debt can be great, if leveraged (we'll talk a lot about that in later chapters). My kids are aware of these things. Even in college, they are teaching the mindset of becoming followers. They're not teaching entrepreneurship, wealth mindset, or how to gain true financial freedom. We have been teaching those things to our kids pretty much from birth.

Beau and I are unified in what we want to instill in our kids. Although the kids are all different, they sure do share a lot of the same personality traits. We want them to be creative thinkers, have open minds and open hearts, to be risk takers and dreamers, and not to be tied into societal norms and expectations. Often, it is a challenge to parent these kiddos, but we wouldn't want it any other way. We've been working on this their entire lives. We want them to be solutionists. When they hit adversity, we ask them, "What are you going to do about this? Are you going to find an answer, or just quit?" We want them to see adversity as opportunity for growth. We teach them the art of negotiation and to never split the difference (all fine and dandy, until they use it on us. Can you say backfire?).

Our kids read a lot of self-help books. A few they've read include:

- *Never Split the Difference* by Christopher Voss,
- *10x is Easier than 2x* by Dan Sullivan,
- *100M Dollar Leads* by Alex Hormozi,
- *How to Win Friends and Influence People* by Dale Carnegie,
- *The Alchemist* by Paolo Coelho, and
- *The Richest Man in Babylon* by George Clason.

Xoë keeps her gratitude journal on her nightstand. She writes down the things she is grateful for every day. We try to raise our kids based on the whole child theory. It's very much the Montessori model. We think about how to raise them based on their interests using inquiry learning. For example, they liked butterflies, so we brought in larvae and watched them grow into beautiful butterflies and then let them go free into the world. That was a great experience. We teach them to manage their feelings, to communicate transparently, and to always try to be good humans.

So now, the kids have visited all the continents on the planet! That was a HUGE family goal and although I was scared shitless to cross that Drake passage between Chile and Antarctica, I had to swallow my fear and do as I preach and get us to the finish line! We are so super jazzed and grateful that we completed this goal together. It was one the most, if not the most, unique times thus far in any of our lives and we have thousands of pictures to prove it. We witnessed and experienced things only a handful of people ever will.

We have created a mission and a vision for our family and try to base all our decisions on those value systems. Thinking out of the normal blocks can sometimes create issues. Our kids are strong willed and can be hyper critical without a filter. (That might be my fault; my filter is nearly non-existent.) They are not concerned as much if they are liked. They aren't into gossip or minutia. They have to search a little harder to find their tribe.

We choose physical activities and educational experiences that no local schools could possibly offer. We believe in classrooms without walls. My kids are multiracial and multicultural, which can come with its own benefits and challenges.

> *We want our kids to be able to walk through the world in their own way, not the way the world expects of them.*

The main thing is we want our kids to be able to walk through the world in their own way, not the way the world expects of them. We hope that we've given them a wide breadth of experiences, ideas, skills, and education, but more importantly, a mindset of possibilities, that all things are possible if you believe in yourself. We don't want them to think that a 9 -to- 5 job is their only option, unless of course they want to. They think about businesses they can start, side hustles, and multiple streams of income. It's not all about money or how much they make. I want them to become millionaires and I want them to be happy, well rounded people who contribute to the world in whatever way suits them. Our hope is that we are raising good, kind, inclusive humans. You have to give them these things; kids aren't born this way. You have to shape the way they see the world and move in it.

You don't have to be rich to do things that will affect your kids' growth. You can simply spend time with them. If you do have big dreams to travel or do cool stuff that costs money, you can engineer ways to save money that you might not have thought of. We put everything on our Amex cards and we pay the card off every month, so we aren't wasting money on high interests. Over the years, we have gained so many points which we use for airline miles so that we rarely pay for plane tickets anymore—we use our miles.

You can do something like camping out in your own back-yard or a local state park. Outdoor activities like walking to-gether, biking, swimming are good exercise and a chance to be without phones and devices that distract from time to just talk or just be together. Cook together as a family, read books or watch movies together and discuss them, learn a language, learn a few. There are apps for that, and most are very affordable, less than $10 a month for many of them. Learning a new language is a great way to ex-pand your mind and will likely make your kids get curious about other cultures and how they live. It will open them up to being more inclusive and tolerant and instill a desire to travel and experience places and people that are differ-ent from what they already know.

We weren't always rich. We couldn't do the things we can do now. It took time, focus, and commitment to our goals to get to this place. It's doable. I know, because we did it, and we are still in the game every day. We made all the mistakes with the kids and with money that lots of young people do. We bought too much crap when we were younger: cars, gadgets, and gifts for the kids that added no real value to their lives (liabilities). We could have used that money to create additional wealth through buying cash flow producing assets instead, but we wised up even-tually. Now we don't buy gifts for birthdays and holidays— if our kids want something, they have the money to buy it. Instead, we buy experiences. We don't buy liabilities; we buy assets. They add value to our lives and we strive to add value to our children. Now that we have created multiple streams of income, we use our passive income to buy those experiences and any liabilities.

Every Christmas, we buy each of us three gifts: something to read, something you need, and something for fun. Then we take our gifts with us on whatever trip we're going on. Our family travels are something none of us will ever forget. These will be with us all for the rest of our lives. We're creating moments and memories for life. There is no greater gift.

We created a mission, vision, and value system for our family, but that's our system. It's not likely going to be the same for you and your family, but you need to create and commit to your own value system. It's important. It's a roadmap for you and the kids.

ACTION ITEMS:

☐ Create a mission statement for yourself as a parent. Why do you do what you do?

☐ What core values lead your family? Generosity, abundance, transparency, kindness?

☐ Think about the funds you'll need to take a trip or create an experience for your family. What are you willing to give up? What are you willing to do to add to your income?

☐ Are you committed to teaching your kids about finances and business? Consider bringing them to business events or enrolling them in an online financial literacy class like Outschool or 10 x kids.

☐ Invest in financial literacy curiosity question games like Cashflow for Kids by Robert Kiyosaki, based on lessons from his New York Times bestseller, *Rich Dad Poor Dad*.

☐ Help them understand money by playing Monopoly—we love that game and play often.

CHAPTER 5

PRIORITIZE ROL (RETURN ON LIFE) VS. ROI

I've found that people get nervous when you talk about budgets. There's a fear around knowing the truth about what you have, what you make, and what you spend. Budgeting is too often something people just don't do, but once you have that budget in place, you can start to consider your return on investment. Your return should not just be on money, but your quality of life. Think about your ROL—Return on Life. You should plan to not only multiply your money but also increase the satisfaction you get from your life—tenfold!

Creating a budget means taking a good hard look at your finances, being vulnerable and transparent, and making a plan. Budgeting for your personal finances is a great way to get a handle on reaching your goals or achieving dreams you might have. Say you want to buy a new car, go on a vacation or are thinking about buying a home; creating a budget is essential. It goes back to starting with the end in mind.

The same thing applies to starting or growing a business. I told you that when I started the first of my Montessori schools, I created a plan and that included a monthly budget. There were definites—rent and scary loan shark payments were always the same and not negotiable. We were able to project things like supplies, food for the kids, and hours for staff. We could make educated guesses based on industry standards. My monthly budget was the forecast for my yearly budget. As Beau and I grew the school business, adding school after school, we had to consider the pro forma for each new school.

By definition, pro forma is a method of calculating financial results of a project or business plan using projections or presumptions of what the end result should be. Knowing how much we wanted each school to yield monthly and yearly, let us create a roadmap to get there. I thought, *Okay, if I'm going to have a successful school, I need to have this many kids, because I have this many expenses.*

I projected or presumed what those expenses would be and then I created a budget based on those numbers. I had to do that with each new school we started. It became easier to make those educated guesses the more we got to be old pros. How many hours we needed for staff, how much food would cost, equipment costs, advertising, and rough guesses on utility bills were things we could be pretty sure of and could account for month by month. Did we get some serious surprises along the way? You bet! We planned for that as well, though.

We were fortunate that we learned a lot from our mentors and we spent a lot of money learning those lessons. When you hear "budget," you might be thinking, Shit, there goes my fun money. NO! Budgets aren't about scarcity. If you love that Starbucks coffee you get every morning that gets you moving, I'm not suggesting that you have to give that up. It's not a $5 beverage that's going to make or break you on a daily, right? It's not the Starbucks. It's the mentality around what got you to the Starbucks. Maybe that one treat is worth it for your life's ROI.

> *Think about your ROL— Return on Life. You should plan to not only multiply your money but also increase the satisfaction you get from your life— tenfold!*

What people don't talk about is that when you're talking about money mindset or having a wealth mindset, we bring so much trauma into the conversation. I get that; I bring issues from my upbringing—the way money was thought of when I was growing up.

Issues from your youth about money don't just go away. You have to work so hard at reframing that stuff. So like, for me, it was save, save, save, save, save, you know, you're going to have a rainy day and when that comes, you're going to have nothing. It was like this constant script running under the hood in my head. This way of thinking was like a threat; the never-ending threat of running out of money.

And so, when you come from that mindset, when later in life you actually have money, you just want to do everything you can with it. The opposite effect happens. You think, *I'm not going to have this forever, right? I should enjoy it while it lasts.* It's not about the $5 Starbucks. For me, it's like, "Well, now that I've made it, I should be able to give myself the things that I worked so hard for, right?" So, the mentality behind it is, "I can make coffee at home for less than five bucks, but it doesn't taste the same. And I want the luxury of not making the coffee." Truth bomb... I freaking go so far as to Uber the Starbucks to my house. That's how "lazy" I am sometimes. The Starbucks is at the end of my block. Sometimes we're like, "Oh my god, we spent so much money on Uber. What the hell, we're totally capable beings. It's literally two minutes from the house."

I weigh what my time is worth though now, and that changes the game—a lot. What is your #ROL!!!?!?

What does a return on life mean? I mean, what is your time worth versus what is the cost? Say I'm working on my book (you know, the one you're reading right now); the Uber guy brings the coffee to my door. I don't have to get up, get dressed, find my car keys, drive to the Starbucks, park the car and schlep the coffee for us back to the house. NO! I'm not stopping to do all that. Uber does their thing and I'm not interrupted. I get my coffee. I continue on with my work. I'm enjoying that luxury and I'm creating much better use of my time or money. Yes, this is a whole mindset. Right? The question is, do you have the money to do that? If you do, fine. If you don't, you may have to adjust your comfort goals.

It all comes down to mindset. You can't have a fixed mindset about money. In fact, you can't have a fixed mindset about anything in life. The mental mindset around money has to vary depending on the situation you're in, what your individual beliefs are, your experiences, and your values around money.

You have to know your mission around money, which will help shape the vision of your ROI, particularly your return on life (ROL), and how you're going to get there. Most people were brought up to follow the path of a scarcity mindset, me included. I had to reprogram my scarcity mindset, the belief that there's never enough money, right? This mindset constantly leads to this fear, which leads to this anxiety around the old story. You're going to lose everything one day. You're not going to have anything. There's going to be no more money. It's finite and you can't get any more. It gives you insecurity around money, and you don't have confidence, so you don't invest. You don't do anything because of this fear. And the fear is created by unrealistic and really poor background knowledge about money and how it works.

There is an abundance of opportunity, abundance of wealth in the world, and abundance of people who can help you get there. Abundance is a team sport. You likely think about money as an individual exchange and a market commodity, right? Look at it this way. If you're going to get wealthy, do what wealthy people do.

Why don't wealthy people typically save? They're not concerned about saving their money. They're investing every single time. They don't have savings accounts. They save to invest! We don't! And so, our mindset has to go from scarcity to abundance and it takes a long time to get there. There's a lot of beliefs that must be eradicated. There's a lot of family history, a lot of money trauma to let go of. My parents lost their business, which caused them to have trauma around money. That money trauma would have been delivered through generations if we hadn't done something to fix it. We didn't want our kids to have that as their legacy mindset. If this is true in your life, you have to be the one to change. It's about the power of one; it just takes one person in your family to change that trajectory.

> *There is an abundance of opportunity, abundance of wealth in the world, and abundance of people who can help you get there. Abundance is a team sport.*

This understanding about money mindset is hard for a lot of people who grew up with the kind of feelings about money that I did. I broke the cycle, and I still fight the built-in money trauma, but I had a different mindset from early on, and I worked hard to change the mindset my family and my environment was passing on to me. Many people never receive the knowledge that there's another way or other ways to look at money. If you don't know, how can you do better? I genuinely believe that you can't improve your financial situation unless you first change your mindset. Mindset leads to the lack of motivation. If you don't gain the knowledge you need about money and how to create abundance, then the reluctance to seek the opportunity for financial growth will hold you back.

Going from a scarcity to an abundance mindset is the first major change you must make, but the second major change, the next step, is to learn to allow for a growth mindset. Because it doesn't matter if you go from scarcity to abundance. If you stop there, that's it! You're not going to go to that next level. When you work your way to this growth mindset, you begin seeing money as something that's earned, something that's learned, and that can improve. You can continue to improve on the earning part. People with a growth mindset really, truly believe that their financial situation is going to change through effort. They believe that things get better exponentially in relation to how much effort they put in. It's not a "set it and let it" plan for your entire portfolio. It's understanding that you have to do something to create wealth and you have to have money to invest. You must have some control over where your money is going. One way or the other, you must make that money so you can invest it in the right vehicle and then your money can make more money for you.

People say, "Well, how do I start?" For starters, you have to have a W2 job or you have to have a business that creates income. I am saying, you must have earned some money that then becomes transformed to invested income or investments to create passive income. I think that there's a lot of perseverance needed. You need patience. You need to keep learning and to understand all the money things running in the background. You need to create multiple strands of income. You need to save money to invest it!

"But Julie, didn't you just say *not* to save? Didn't you say that rich people don't have savings accounts?" Okay, yeah, I did say that, but I'm not suggesting you have nothing in the bank to save your butt in a pinch. I also said RICH people don't save, they invest (because they have disposable or extra income to invest). I think you need to have at least three months of expenses saved in a high-yield interest account, especially if you own a business (let's think back to that dreaded Covid disaster). That money doesn't get touched unless it's a genuine emergency. It's the safety net that'll catch us if the shit hits the fan. Back when Beau still worked, if he were to lose his job, or he would get sick, or something would happen, at that time, his was the main income. So, we would not have been able to afford three months of our house payments or anything with me trying to use his work checks to pay people. So, you do need a safety net, and you should never rely on credit or debt to have that safety net.

People with a growth mindset are more likely to seek out people to help them with financial growth and opportunity. They're not afraid to ask questions. They are always learning more. As for us, we have paid almost $300,000 in financial and real estate mentorships. We're talking next level!! We spend a lot of money to create, not only money returns, but tax strategies, incentives for saving, and keeping money in our pocket versus handing it to the IRS. So, the effort that we put in is great. It's not like we just sit here and all of a sudden, this just happens to us. That's not how it works. We create inertia or momentum that creates opportunities for action. Many people think it just happens out of nowhere. Somehow, I was given this brilliant mind on financial literacy. Not true. We take this effort, this very intentional effort, to grow our money. We're always learning. We're constantly educating ourselves. It absolutely requires perseverance, and trust me, this stuff is tough. Putting in the minimal effort isn't going to do it. Patting yourself on the back for doing a little something isn't the same as doing something all the time. Consistency is key: the small consistent steps every single day, with no days off.

It's important to be reviewing your financial plan all the time. Where are you at? Where do you want to go? Are you aligned with your goals? And are you with people that are going to help you get to your goal? Because people (and relationships) are a huge component that we don't always consider. Did you know that 99 percent of your success comes from your "reference group" (the people you associate with) and 85 percent of our happiness comes from our relationships!

To really see and review and have a clear reference point of where you are at financially, please download, print, and fill out the personal financial statement at this link: https://www.score.org/resource/template/personal-financial-statement-template

You might do this with your accountant.

> *When you hang out with winners, you start winning too.*

You have to think about life changes, right? Where are you in your life right now and what type of life changes may happen to you? For some, it's marriage, starting a family, a big career change, or an economic shift, like we just had. I think you must adjust your financial energy and strategy continuously. You should seek professional advice and meet with somebody that can help you with that strategy, but I admit, I'm not a huge fan of financial advisors that are tied to specific funds, so seeking out a CPA (certified public accountant) who is well-versed in creating financial plans might be best. We used a few different folks to define ours. But you do need a financial plan, and that requires discipline. If you don't have discipline with your financial projections or your financial plan, you're not going to get anywhere. Making a plan and not following it is pointless. Kind of like that action/no action thing. It works the same way. Your financial plan needs to be personalized to the lifestyle you want. Staying the path takes a lot of effort. You need to put effort in and stay on top of things, which means you need consistent evaluation. You need to check your actual results against the plan. What are you doing? Are you getting there? Is this working for you? What needs tweaking? What's working and what is not?

If you can't increase your income, inevitably, you need to change your lifestyle. Something's got to give, right? It's got to be one side or the other. So, if you want to live the way you want to live, then you have to create a next level of income. That's if you want to keep moving. If not, then you stay where you're at, but inflation and everything else is going to continue with or without you. To be real, you're just going to get more inundated by less value in your life.

You must believe in yourself, and you must know that you can absolutely learn the skills needed to become an expert. Most importantly, you have to do the work and get the education, and put in the time to become effectual at your profession.

To increase your ROL, invest in yourself. Did you know? "It takes the average person 10,000 hours to become an expert at something." Investing in yourself is one of the most valuable investments you will ever make. Continuous learning and self-improvement leads to professional growth and development. Expertise in your industry sets you apart from others and gives you a highly competitive edge, especially if you're an entrepreneur. It gives you instant and increased credibility while creating trust.

HOW TO BECOME AN ROL EXPERT:

Set clear goals. Define what you want to be an expert in and measure your growth in order to achieve it.

Keep learning. Enroll in courses, workshops, and sessions with masterminds. Read books. Watch YouTube.

Practice. Apply what you learn to your everyday.

Network. Tony Robbins says, "Proximity is Power." Follow that!

Stay updated. Keep up with all the news, trends and on the what's what of your industry today.

I didn't always know about how to effectively run a business, how to increase profits, expand quickly and efficiently, or how to create legacy wealth through real estate investments. I did put the time in, though. I did get in those rooms. I prayed I was the least knowledgeable one there so I could learn everything and take immediate action. I got super hyper-focused about my goals and mastered them one at a time. My intention was to create inertia. I knew I needed momentum to create this flow. I did everything to become an expert at everything I did, and that was the game changer right there. I wasn't a master of all trades, but I did become the master of ONE trade at a time.

Every decision you make makes you, because at the end of the day, you're responsible. You make 100 percent of the decisions for your life. When you wake up, you decide something and part of that is showing up—showing up for your family, your clients or customers, and for yourself.

ACTION ITEMS:

- ☐ Create a budget for your business and your personal life.

- ☐ What money trauma is holding you back? How do you plan to overcome it?

- ☐ Do you have an abundant mindset? Or a scarcity mindset?

- ☐ Do you have a routine? What can you commit to every day to move you toward your North Star (your ultimate goal)?

- ☐ Are you consistent with your efforts?

- ☐ Do you have checks/balances in place to measure against?

- ☐ What is one thing you can do today to change the trajectory of your tomorrow?

- ☐ Who is your mentor? In life, business, health, mindset or other?

- ☐ Are you thinking big enough? If no, why not?

CHAPTER 6

INCREASE YOUR INCOME

I love my coach, Grant Cardone. He told me early on, "You don't have an expense problem. You have an income problem." His reasoning was that most expenses are fixed. When you own your home, you can't control your taxes. You can't really control the cost of your utilities (well, you can shut off lights and lower air conditioning or heat, but mostly, it's out of your hands). You can't control a lot of those fixed expenses. What you have to control is how much money you're making. If you want to buy that house or start that business, maybe you need to create a side hustle. Maybe you need a Plan B to create external revenue streams. You might need passive income streams. But at the end of the day, the expense problem is not the problem. It's the income problem.

If you want more things, better things, or you're not living at the standard you want, then raise your income. The control, at its core, is how much you're bringing in, what your income level is, or your revenue, whether that's business or personal. That goal should be the driving force to create and guide your financial planning process. Setting clear goals is number one, next is creating income, then finally, assessing risk and creating a plan. Obviously, you have to create a budget to track your income versus your expenses.

For the schools, we tracked our income in a very particular way. We would create a spreadsheet of... here's what's coming in for revenue and then here are the industry standard percentages for all of our expenses. Then we asked, are we within those acceptable percentages?

So, if our revenue was a million dollars a year, our payroll, at that time, followed the industry standard, which was 50 percent. The rest of the expenses followed a percentage of revenue as well. Then we would ask, "Where are we in relation to that?" The answer to any questions of profitability was the net revenue. At the time, the building needs should have fallen between 12 percent and 16 percent of revenue to be in line with industry standards. We looked at where we were for that. To create a budget based on industry standards, you do a little research. That kind of information is easily found. We learned a lot of those industry standards by attending industry conferences and learning from industry-based mastermind group and by consistently pouring into ourselves.

This is the way you can check out if you're in the realm of where you should be. By creating the expected budget—back to pro forma—you can decide if you're creating a business or a job for yourself. Are you creating a revenue stream that has a net income, or are you buying yourself a job? And so knowing all those pieces, identifying areas where you can reduce some expenses, or save, the main thing, though, is going to be about your income. How much money you have coming in, where you need to put it, and where it's being spent. At the end of the day, are you within a budget that allows you to be really financially successful, not just grinding away without viable profit. If you aren't making over 20 percent in profit, you're inevitably just buying yourself a job with a huge amount of risk and liability attached.

With the schools, we didn't want to create a job for ourselves. We wanted to grow and scale a profitable business that served our clientele with a highly valuable and exceptional product. You need to know your numbers every day. By planning, learning, budgeting, by putting in the right policies and procedures, we were able to create businesses that made real profits every month and all year long. We had a nice model of recurring revenue. The most highly sought-after businesses for private equity purchase are built on a model of recurring revenue.

During Covid, one of my clients had a big loss of income, as did lots of people. She had to think out of the box and her comfort zone to stay afloat. She taught art classes and was used to having lots of students at her in-person classes and after-school programs. So, we pivoted. We came up with the idea of her putting together art kits and delivering them to the students. She would leave a package on each kid's porch with supplies and a video. The parents and kids would watch the video and do the project. It was much needed relief from the boredom these kids were facing, as well as gave the parents some relief. She is still doing that even now that she is open for regular business. She has the students pick up the supplies and activity kits now on her porch and it gives the family something to do on a rainy afternoon or low-key weekend. They download the video now and work with the art supplies provided.

Obviously, her art classes are now full, so it is also a great way to keep wait-listed kiddos engaged with her!

There's a common misconception with lots of people that if they could just cut expenses, they would be more successful. This pertains to both personal and business expenses.

Cutting out things like comfort items, massages, pedicures, nights out eating dinner, the ever-popular Starbucks (I am addicted), might save a little money, but the thing is, you can't cut everything. You can't turn off the water or the electricity. And do you want to? Will cutting stuff out increase your ROL (return on life) or deplete it? I think you know the answer to that.

If you own a business, you might find some expenses can be reduced, but what will that do to your reputation if those products lessen the quality of your work? You wouldn't use cheap house paint if you're a painter or cheap burger meat if you're a burger joint. Your clients will recognize the drop in quality and that means less referrals and less repeat business.

Your problem isn't about your expenses, it's about your income. If you want to be more successful in business, more comfortable in your lifestyle, and provide a better life for your family, you simply have to make MORE money. But how?

It's easier to add services for existing clients than it is to get new ones. We learned this and made it happen at the schools. We knew if we added services that added convenience and value to our parents, it would mean added revenue. We found things that brought us more income without any more actual work. That is the real goal if you can achieve it. Partnering with shoulder industries and getting your referral fee brings more value to your existing clients and more money to your bottom line. In essence, that was what we did. We didn't teach music or piano, but we ran schools. Music teachers were a kind of shoulder industry partner—still teaching, right? Without having to learn piano or pay more music teachers, we offered the classes as an option and the teacher paid us part of what she made from those small group lessons. Cha-ching! No more work, just added revenue streams! Finding ways to utilize the services of people who do something that you don't do BUT that your clients want can bring in that extra income.

Once you've exhausted ways to serve existing clients by offering as many possible additional things to them you can think of, if you need more revenue, you may have to create multiple streams of income. If you offer a service, like my caterer, what other services can you offer that your existing clients will want? Can you do some event planning, wedding planning? If you're a graphic artist, can you learn to make websites? It might take some training, but rather than handing clients over to someone else, you can offer to take their artwork and make a WordPress, Wix, or Squarespace site.

Maybe you simply need more clients. What can bring you new clients? Can you increase your marketing or target a new avatar that will increase sales and the bottom line? Do you need to get the word out more about what you do and who you serve? Networking, getting on podcasts, talking about what you do every chance you get takes effort, but it pays off. Sometimes it takes a little more grinding to get more clients.

Have you considered white labeling your services to other companies? Client acquisition is one of the most expensive parts of doing business. If someone else can get you the client, it might be worthwhile to offer that business owner a discount on your services, so there's room in the end cost for the client. You offer a discount of 20 percent or so to a company that has clients in your space, and they can make that percentage by selling your services to those clients. Yes, you make a little less on those transactions, but these are clients you wouldn't have gotten. Offering referral fees to people can bring in extra clients. This incentive can bring new clients from out of the box places.

The need to increase income instead of giving shit up is why people have side hustles. Uber, Lyft, Instacart, and services like that exist on the backs of people who are working at those services more often than not as a side hustle. Realtors when the market slows down, hospitality professionals during slow seasons, and sadly, teachers on nights and weekends, will drive for Uber or deliver food. If that's what it takes, you do it! If you need to create a side hustle, there is a word of caution, though. Don't let the side hustle allow you to take your eye off the main game or goal. Your primary business must stay your north star. Focus is important. If you find yourself delivering food more than selling houses, you might want to rethink the side hustle.

If you work a corporate gig but want to be a business owner, you might start the business you want to be in as a side hustle that will lead to a full-time business. Do NOT give up your W2 JOB until you have the new business making money. After all, money is money is money.

Lots of people who want to be coaches, consultants, or speakers make this mistake. They might write a book, get a few gigs talking about their primary subject matter skill, and make the jump too soon. Write the book nights and weekends. Take a day or two off if you get a paid speaking gig, but don't give up a salary and benefits until you have paying, recurring clients and recurring loyalty from those clients. You need to know they are solid; they are staying with you, and referring you to others to help you grow. It's a bridging process. You have to build the bridge first before you step out into thin air.

Starting a business requires money. Making money requires money! Keep that job and you can start investing in the new business as well as save for the money your business will require you to have in the future (Remember how we used Beau's paychecks to pay teachers in the early days... this is exactly why I am cautioning you!).

The great thing here is that we've made all the mistakes. We have been entrepreneurs for the past 30 years now. It is not an easy gig, folks!! The sheer stamina, endurance, and mental and physical grit that you must have is second to no ironman. We will compress your success timeline even by just simply offering you "what not-to's"!

> *Do NOT give up your W2 JOB until you have the new business making money. After all, money is money is money. You have to build the bridge first before you step out into thin air.*

It will mean a lot of work after your paid job day is over. But it's worth it if you want to be a coach, teach courses, get paid to speak and... in the long run, likely make as much or more money than you do at the job with a lot more freedom.

BONUS: IGNITING YOUR ENTREPRENEURIAL SPARK! A GUIDE TO LAUNCHING YOUR SMALL BUSINESS

If you have a successful business that is up and running, you can skip this bonus section if you want. But if you are in a W2 JOB and are thinking about starting a business either as a side hustle or to move into when leaving your position, I wanted to share some things that might be helpful for you to know or at least think about.

Let's start with the basics.

General outline of steps to your first business (this is a whole other book, so I'm going to just lightly touch on the order of operations).

16. Define your vision, identify your core values, and craft your business concept

17. Do market research and analysis (demographic research, competition, target customers)

18. Create your Business Blueprint (road map or business plan)

19. Learn about the various business structures and find the right one for your business

20. Secure financing (options available and securing funds)

21. Build your brand (marketing, website, marketing campaigns, social media presence)

22. Launch your business (physical space, location)

23. Ongoing financial management and budgeting

24. Embrace a solution-based mindset

25. Reap the rewards of entrepreneurship

The main thing is just DO IT! So many people talk about starting a business. They think about it. They research and plan and... NEVER START! The expression, *build the plane in the air*, applies. I'm not saying go off blindly and invest tons of money and time, quit your job, and jump off a business cliff with no parachute. What I am saying is, set up the LLC and do the things that you can afford that will get you started. It might mean making a simple logo, setting up some social media, and testing the waters. See what people are interested in. When you start to get a little traction, you get some clients or customers, then build the next thing. Might be a website, might be taking ads, setting up a course, or writing a course, a book or a workbook. Do one thing, then do the next, and the next.

You don't need to find your ultimate purpose in life. I am not a fan of that concept. When people say they can't get started because they haven't figured out their "purpose," I ask, "What kind of purpose? Financial, family, health?" Your business should be something that excites you, that makes you want to jump out of bed and get going in the morning. Think about what you're good at, what you love to do, who your business will serve and help, and then take the first step. You don't have to know everything. You need to get the right people around you. You can ask for advice, seek help, research, and grow on the job.

> *Just start! Take action and figure it out. The expression, build the plane in the air, applies.*

Just start! Take action and figure it out. Remember, people who never take action, never get results. You might think that you can never fail if you never try, but that's a lie people tell themselves.

The real failure is in never trying.

What skills do you have that can make you money? If you like sales and are good at it, there are people who actually make money with network or affiliate marketing companies. If you're already buying healthy foods and beauty aids, why not get paid for it? There are good network and affiliate marketing companies that can save you money on high-quality products and can make you money when you "sell" the idea of joining to other people. Network marketing is NOT for everyone, but for people who get into it, it can be very lucrative and it can be done while you still work at the corporate gig.

If you're the type of person who likes doing more than one thing, starting a cottage industry business as a side hustle is super popular and might be for you. You might have a great recipe for granola, hot sauce, jam or jelly, or breads like banana or peach. Everyone says you should sell those. We know a woman who makes amazing pound cake, and she sells it as a side hustle. Her clients are corporate folks and realtors who want to impress clients. She has molds to make the pound cake in different shapes (get your mind out of the gutter) and she puts your logo on the box. When the person receives your gift, it's very personal. She gets a lot per pound cake, but they are unique and worth the cost. She has a regular gig as well, but this is something she loves to do and it makes her as much money as her day job.

Some people make soap or candles, candy or popcorn. There are lots of cottage industries, but you have to know the rules. Every state has rules about what you can sell, who you can sell to (many don't allow you to sell to restaurants), what kind of environment you have to have to create your goodies, like you might need to rent space in a commercial kitchen, and how much money you're allowed to make each year. Be sure to look up the laws in your state before you waste money on building this hustle.

Whatever you do to make that extra money, as long as it's legal and valuable, is way better than trying to cut out things you want, love, or, in some cases, need. We are ALWAYS working, thinking of new ways to increase our income. We love our lifestyle. We're not giving that up. We would rather just be proactive, hustle, learn, and grow. Our kids are always thinking of business ideas, side hustles, and multiple streams of income. If one thing slips, the other thing rises. It requires brainstorming, staying up with trends, and, in our case, investing. Sometimes you have to borrow money to make money, but there are rules to that too.

ACTION ITEMS:

☐ Identify at least three complementary or compatible revenue streams to add to your business and bring in revenue.

☐ Identify at least three community referral partners that you can work with. A restaurant might try pairing with a movie or community theater for a ticket to the show and dinner.

☐ Introduce yourself to members of the community with a small gift—a tin of cookies maybe—and let them know what you do. Ask if there are ways you can help them with what they need.

☐ Sponsor community events to gain community trust—this does not have to only mean local events. There are many online events to sponsor, especially if you belong to an online group or community.

CHAPTER 7

BUILD AN EXCEPTIONAL CUSTOMER EXPERIENCE

Whether you're a solopreneur, a small business, or a large corporation, you will very likely have competition. Unless you have invented a whole new product or industry, other people will very likely be doing the same thing you are (or copying what you're doing as soon as they figure it out), offering the same kinds of services. To stand out from the crowd, you have to be exceptional.

But what does it mean to be exceptional? How do you get there?

I always saw our Montessori preschool as a business we would want to grow. My why wasn't financial, though—it was to provide an exceptional preschool program to as many children as we could. My why was **IMPACT**. As I look back on many of my business ventures, they all have one thing in common: I wanted a large scale impact for others. One school was great, but that wasn't the ultimate plan. That wasn't enough. I knew we would grow beyond that and to do that, we had to be different. We had to be better than everyone else. We had to be stand-out phenomenal. Knowing that and implementing ways to be exceptional was the first step to go from one school to two then to five to ten, and so on. Once we had the model, it became easier to replicate it and even improve on it school by school.

> *If you want to be exceptional, you have to believe you can be! You have to want it and, like us, you have to be obsessed about the success of your business.*

Part of being exceptional was continually seeking ways to add more services, more value for our community and clients. What I promised the parents of my Montessori Preschools was, "You're going to get a high-level, amazing, exceptional early learning program, plus you're not going to run around all over the place to get all the extra stuff for your kids. I'm going to take care of that. WE GOT YOU!" I gave them value galore and, in the process, created tons of external revenue generating options for us.

We made our customers' lives easier by adding things that saved them time, effort, and sometimes, even money. We did summer care, after-school care, and before-school care. We offered hot lunches. We offered extra sporting activities, like soccer, for our students. Parents loved that they could have this right at the school for their child. They would sign up their kids, the soccer people would come to the school, and we got a revenue share. We did a music program. The parents were like, "Sign me up!" And... we got a revenue share. We decided we would have uniforms at one of the schools. You guessed it, we got a revenue share, right from the uniform sales company. We did Mandarin classes, after school robotics, all kinds of add-ons and yup... revenue share! None of this cost us any extra money out of pocket. We didn't have to market it beyond telling our existing clients, the parents, that we had all this cool stuff they wanted for their kids. We were able to offer this by pairing up with amazing services for children in our community, all while adding value and no extra amount of work for us.

It's easy to understand how this impacted our schools. Parents hang out with other parents. They have friends, siblings, cousins, or co-workers with kids in similar age brackets. Once you build exceptional value, they tell the people in their circle about you.

Here are some additional ways in which we added increased value to our clients:

We offered a contracted subscription. Our clients signed a yearlong contract and renewed each year with a price increase (hedged against inflation). This way, we knew the base income expected each month for the year.

We packaged product "bundles" or services together at a discounted price. Clients who paid for the full year upfront got 10 percent off tuition and activities. It is always easier to sell more to an engaged customer than trying to acquire a new one.

We used and got great at email marketing. A CRM is a must. We used Line Leader, and for our real estate platform, we now use Go High Level.

We personalized all interactions with our customers. We created relationships.

We created a referral program. I was happy to give referral fees to people who would bring in business. Lots of businesses will do that, and it's a great way to show appreciation to your client.

We committed to continuous improvement and always delivered incredible customer service.

We built trust and loyalty. In every business venture, our focus is always on transparency, integrity, and building long-term, mutually beneficial relationships with clients.

To deliver an exceptional customer experience, you must constantly be in add-on mode. But remember: the services or products you add should complement what you already offer. You're not just going to add some rando thing that has nothing to do with what you're already offering. That's not thinking smart. It has to relate to your primary service or product to make sense or it won't likely sell. And obviously, you need to know the risk versus reward profile of anything you do.

We have pulled this mentality into our coaching conversations with business owners wanting to expand. With each of our investors, I want to know, "What do you need? What do you want? How can we help? How can we add value?"

If you can't add value, then you might as well not be having a conversation.

I currently offer business consulting, and one of my clients is a young lady who just put a course together from a book she wrote. She made a ton of money selling that one course. And she's going to continue to use that course to branch off into other courses and related services and products. But I was like, "Well, okay, so now, let's create a subscription process and a community. We can have them funnel into your new community, and this subscription process is going to capture what you're doing in the course." When people become part of the community, they get all these additional things. The community doesn't have to be expensive, but once you create the subscription process, or from the course, or the book, or whatever it is, this new community will be happy to pay you for insider ideas. They want your expert insider tips and tricks. Additional streams of revenue—same customer!

No matter what type of business you have, you must think about things that both add value to existing customers and increase your revenue. Say you own a family-friendly restaurant. What's hot and trending? Barbie! Restaurants are typically slow between lunch and dinner. So why not offer birthday parties from 3 to 5 PM? Create themed birthday party packages, featuring Barbie or Teenage Mutant Ninja Turtles, so you can benefit from all the hype on social media and TV. You have everything already food-wise or you can make some simple offerings. Make pink soda for Barbie using grenadine and lemon soda. Buy a cheap pink carpet for the little girls to walk in on. Make pink cupcakes. Serve pizza for the turtles, and add green food coloring to cupcake icing. Most dollar stores or party stores will have things like cups and paper plates with themes for the hot kids' movie of the month. Create simple games to play and put your most fun and personable server on the gig. Your lunch and dinner crowd likely has kids or grandkids. Come up with ideas to bring them in while you're slow. It beats cutting expenses like letting servers go or giving them less hours, cutting costs with cheaper products, or closing on slow days. Be creative! Just find ways to ADD VALUE AND MAKE MORE MONEY.

To build an exceptional customer experience, most business owners realize they can't go it alone. Beau and I could have run one small school by ourselves. We might have even grown a little by having one or two employees and made enough to live a quiet, simple life. That isn't us!

So, first and foremost, we had to find and hire exceptional people—people who shared our vision and dedication enough to grow with us. Not all of them stayed on the team, but the ones that did helped us as we grew. The ones who became integral team members were held accountable. They didn't mind this—in fact, they wanted that accountability. It made their job easier in the long run. To expand the way we did, the people we hired became more and more critical. They were family, and we treated them as such.

As we grew, we learned that we had to be willing to pivot, change, reevaluate, add, and delete things. We knew that being stagnant was not the path to growth. We constantly educated ourselves. We learned new trends; we tried new things; we embraced failing faster and learning what worked. We paid to learn from the best mentors!

We created systems and processes, and we were flexible when implementing them. We listened to our team and embraced their input and feedback! That's a big one. We listened to our staff, our parents, and even our students. When they showed us that some things about our systems needed to change, we accepted that change had to happen. This helped us create loyal customers, who in turn wanted to help us grow. Vulnerability was key.

We created Key Performance Indicators (KPIs) for ourselves and our employees. Those key metrics let us measure our success and helped us to make informed business decisions. We used these KPIs to measure our performance and see if we were meeting the objectives we set for the business, our staff, and ourselves. We were motivated by excellence.

And the hardest part—we had to learn to give up control. I struggled with this. Of course, ultimately, we were in control of the entire operation, but we, especially I, had to learn to trust that other people were doing their work, handling their responsibilities, and not micro-manage everyone and everything. Micro managers stay in micro businesses. You need to inspect but not control everything.

> *Micro managers stay in micro businesses.*

To grow a successful business, you need to stand out and capture that exceptional piece of the market. If you don't stand out, then you just fit in. You are just another business, vendor, enterprise like all the rest. If you aren't doing the things that create an exceptional customer experience, you blend in with every other business in your field. The more you get out there, the more you're out in the community, the faster you become a household name. Warning, you have to have a solid reputation to start with. Your reputation will precede and follow you. Start by being good humans, good employers, give exceptional service, and high value to your clients. Lots of companies can say they do that but it's the same old same old. Rhetoric about how great your services are often sound like everyone else's marketing claims. Having a larger market share helps brand you in the community and helps when you're ready to grow. We have lots more tricks to offer you on this in our courses (They could each be a book in and of themselves).

While building our exceptional Montessori schools, we made a name for ourselves in the community by sponsoring everything we possibly could—hockey teams, soccer teams, and parades. We lined up a Santa for the town kids at Christmas and gave out gifts. I spent time at our local hospital delivering toys to kids with cancer and overnight care packages to the new moms in the neo-native care units. We would get tins of muffins or treats and bring them to other local companies to thank them for their service. We did a ton of reciprocal marketing—sharing our message and the message of like-minded businesses together. Being an integral part of the community matters. I was the gold sponsor for every event, paying for the top-level sponsorships and showing up to talk about the schools. All these things mattered. People, and not just our clients, thought of us as a community support system not just a business. For us, that made sense. We had a physical location in towns that we could become known in easily. All it took was time, effort, and serious commitment.

> *If you don't stand out, then you just fit in. You are just another business, vendor, enterprise like all the rest...Every decision you make, makes you.*

Even if you are more of an online business, national and even international, you can make yourself known. You can be exceptional in your service and commitment. You can sponsor online events, summits, and networking conferences. Be the go-to for advice and knowledge in your field of expertise. I'm not saying give the house away, but becoming a trusted source for other business owners in your circles can be the game changer for growing quickly

Finally, creating an exceptional business takes putting in exceptional personal effort. My daily routine includes being intentional with my time and focusing on and prioritizing which things I need to take action on first. I have to send out so many emails a day. I have to make sure we're staying on top of the marketing component. I must market myself and what we are achieving every single day. Nearly every day, I write valuable posts for social media and no, believe it or not, it's not always something I look forward to doing, but I need to give my people value!

Marketing yourself, obviously, is super, super, super important and what you put out there can bring attention in lots of ways. I said something recently that really hit home for a lot of people. It got a lot of attention. ***Every decision you make, makes you***. That one statement hit home for people. Tell people who you are, what you believe in. Show up. That's part of marketing. You are your business. One of my mentors, Grant Cardone, said to me, "The single most important job of the CEO is to market themselves!" Game changer.

Put in the time. I don't even know how many webinars I'm on each week. I'm constantly asked to be on other people's podcasts, I'm constantly listening to podcasts, and constantly on Zoom calls at night. Sometimes, there are three calls on at the same time, and sometimes I have my computer on and I'm listening to something on my phone to make sure I'm not missing stuff. Consistent commitment and effort are required. You need to show up every single day.

When you consider the needs of the same clients, you already have and create more customer value, you increase the value for you too. That value equates to the added creation of revenue for you and the added creation of value for them. Those clients will stick with you, and they will be your allies. You're offering lifetime customer value and legacy value. They will refer you to everyone down the line. Lots of Montessori School kids grow up, and guess what? They have kids and where do you think they're going to send their kids to school? The more value you add, the better your chances to create a strong business, even a legacy business, that outlives you!

ACTION ITEMS:

☐ Define what makes you and your company stand out. How do you measure your exceptionalism? Who is accountable?

☐ Take an intentional look at what your current customer value is. Then, make a concerted effort to increase by 10 percent.

☐ What product or service bundles can you create to add value for your existing clients?

☐ Do you market yourself? How consistently? Do you have a marketing plan?

☐ Look at opportunities to partner in your community. What can you do to give back and stand out?

CHAPTER 8

KNOW THE 5 C'S OF YOUR CREDIT

To borrow or not to borrow? That is the question! Thinking that credit is more money for you to spend is a common mistake. I get at least a hundred offers for credit cards and loans every month, which head straight to the recycle bin. The mistake people often make is thinking, "Cool, I just got a new credit card with a high limit. I can spend some (or all of that) on myself." Credit cards have to be paid back, like all loans. The credit card companies make their money from interest. They all have extremely high interest rates; that is their business model. Using that money for liabilities (wants like clothes and things that don't cash flow) is wasteful. There are reasons to borrow money, but there are rules to it as well.

" *Credit cards have to be paid back, like all loans.*

Loans can be useful and can be helpful when you're trying to reach certain growth or expansion goals, but they must be paid back. If the interest rates and the terms make sense, then borrow. We have borrowed lots of money for investments in the past when the interest rate was 2 percent and the cap was 5 percent. Now, the interest rate is 8 percent and the cap 5 percent . We would be upside down if we borrowed money for purchases, so now we buy cash. Calculate the loan you're considering carefully. Weigh the cost over the benefits of borrowing. If it makes sense, do it.

I use a credit card only EVERY DAY FOR EVERYTHING.

Say whattttt???? Why?

POINTS, my friends!! We travel extensively (we are a large family of six) and we use our points constantly for plane tickets, hotels, experiences, etc. However, we reconcile the credit card on the 30th of every month. We do a bank reconciliation through ACH transfer from our checking accounts directly to the credit card company. We pay no interest and use our Apple Pay or our credit card for every single purchase. This tracks everything for the accountants as well. We don't have store credit cards (except for a Scheels Visa as my husband is obsessed with all things Scheels and they give us back mucho dinero $$ on his hunting hobby supplies and that stuff isn't cheap. So we've ok'd that one dept store card. Again, we fully pay that card each month!!).

We have a business **platinum AMEX** with **no limit and a DELTA Reserve card**. There are months we will put up to $100,000 on these cards (property insurances, due diligence items, our groceries, kids' college tuition, and daily living expenses. Honestly, everything we can use it for, we do! We're super sad when they say no credit cards/must be ACH only. We think about all the points that could have given us!), then we reconcile for business or personal purchases (two separate spreadsheets). We determine which card to use based on whether we have reached diamond flying status or not yet on our Delta card. Once we reach status, we switch to the Amex Platinum card as the points can be used for anything on a 1:1 exchange! **We spend less than 1 percent a year in cash**. If we couldn't pay back what we spent in a month, though, we would never do it. So, we don't buy more than we know we have. Only use your credit cards like this if you have the control and can pay them off each month.

There are all types of loans: business, personal, SBA, credit cards, and even HELOCs, which are home equity loans. We used our HELOC to buy our last Tesla. When we buy cars, we buy them in December so we can write the entire depreciation off for the year we are in (6,000 lb. rule), and then we pay the HELOC off putting half the payment on in December and the other half in January. That way, we can max out what we were able to put on that card in both years. There are little tricks to borrowing, but you must know them and well, and if you don't, get a mentor who can help walk you through this.

No matter what type of loan you're looking to secure, you will want to know what lenders base their decisions on.

There are five basic things they consider.

The 5 C's of Credit

1. CHARACTER

Lenders look at your character—meaning your credit history. They can track your record in terms of borrowing and returning. There are three credit bureaus that monitor how you borrow and pay on time: TransUnion, Equifax, and Experian. These generate a FICO score used by lenders as a snapshot of your credit worthiness, particularly the likelihood that you will be paying back on time. That's a big one and speaks to your character in the credit world. They use that score to set the terms and rate you get. The higher the risk, the more terms and higher the rate. Even on an excellent rate basis with a good credit score, right now, interest rates are high. Banks borrow the money to lend out and there is no low rate right now.

In case you were wondering: FICO is an abbreviation for the Fair Isaac Corporation. Bill Fair and Earl Isaac are the founders of the company, which was the first to offer a credit-risk model with a score.

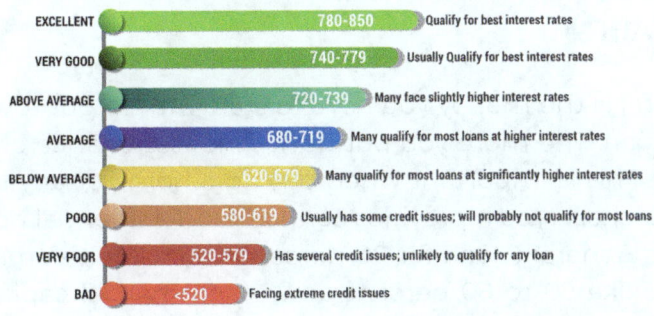

EXCELLENT	780-850	Qualify for best interest rates
VERY GOOD	740-779	Usually Qualify for best interest rates
ABOVE AVERAGE	720-739	Many face slightly higher interest rates
AVERAGE	680-719	Many qualify for most loans at higher interest rates
BELOW AVERAGE	620-679	Many qualify for most loans at significantly higher interest rates
POOR	580-619	Usually has some credit issues; will probably not qualify for most loans
VERY POOR	520-579	Has several credit issues; unlikely to qualify for any loan
BAD	<520	Facing extreme credit issues

2. CAPACITY

Before you get a personal loan, the bank or lender will measure your DTI, debt to income ratio—how much debt you have compared to your income. Take your total monthly debt divided by your monthly income and you will get your DTI. The lower the DTI, the better the chance to qualify for a new loan. Generally, this should be 36 percent or less for approval for personal loans and mortgages.

For commercial loans, they look at your DSCR—Debt Service Cover Ratio. This is pretty low right now—1.2 to 1.25 percent. Basically, the lender wants to know that you have enough income in the business to cover the loan every month. People ask how to improve their capacity. It goes back to the last chapter—increase in income. Add revenue streams, take a second job or start a side hustle. The extra income needs to be stable, though. By that I mean, say you're freelancing and the work is sporadic. A lender might not consider that stable enough to bring in steady, reliable income to bolster the loan. Something too seasonal or that doesn't bring in about the same amount every month is not a good bet for the lender.

3. CAPITAL

Capital is the money you have to start with to put toward the loan. The more you put down, the less chance of default. This is important when buying a home or any larger purchases, as it provides confidence. Residential home loans generally look for 20 percent down. Multi-family is more like 50 to 60 percent down. Commercial capital is more, and the interest rate is killing this. It makes it hard to pay it back. The more capital you have in though, the more they will loan you. It means less risk for the bank.

4. COLLATERAL

Stuff you own that's worth something is collateral. You want to buy assets that will appreciate, like a house, a building, or land. Even a car can be collateral. It makes it easier when securing the loan because if you default they can repo the car, the house, that apartment complex, etc. It's less risky for the lender.

Unsecured loans like an SBA for a new business have higher rates because the lender has no idea if the business will succeed or go under. There is no collateral.

5. CONDITIONS

These are things that can affect the amount of the loan and the ability to pay it back. Banks look at things like the length of time you have been at your job or the kind of business you are in, and the projections for that kind of business. Also, they consider uncontrollable conditions like the economy, legislature, global and political climates, and the value of the dollar.

If you can predict future interest based on the type of business and success in the industry, that could help make the lender more confident in loaning the money.

Bottom line: getting clear about credit will help you steer clear of debt!

ACTION ITEMS:

☐ Check your credit score regularly, and know your FICO score too.

☐ Don't borrow money if you can't pay it back. Not paying those loans can ruin your credit in the long-term. Pay your entire credit card balance every month and on time.

☐ Don't get loans to repay loans. This applies to credit cards too. The bouncing cards game eventually catches up with you. No robbing Peter to pay Paul, funny stuff!

☐ Does your credit card offer rewards? If not, shop around. Find the card with the best rewards for your personal needs.

☐ Comparison shop loans. Don't assume all loans are the same. Get quotes. Ask what the fees are, read all of the terms. Is it variable/fixed, length of term, interest rates/application fees, and prepayment penalties?

CHAPTER 9

AN ASSET CAN BE A LIABILITY

Most of our lives, we've been told that we should own stuff. And I'm not saying that's a bad thing, as it has served us well. But sometimes, it's better for us to ignore that advice. Society tells us to raise our kids like sheep. We tell them to do the same things—go to college, get a W2 job, buy a house with a white picket fence, and own a car, a pool, a dog, and other stuff! This defines who you are... supposedly!

I don't know about you, but all my life I have been told that I needed to own my home. "No one can kick you out of your home. It's security!" Our parents wanted us to have stuff paid outright (at least the status stuff: a house, car, you get what I'm putting down). To them, this is what made you successful. You own things—you've made it.

Try not paying the mortgage or taxes and see how long you get to stay in that house. Owning your home has a feel good element, but remember, houses are in need of constant maintenance. You need to repaint, landscape, cut grass, buy chemicals for the pool, stuff breaks etc.. Don't pay your car loan, and you will look out the window one morning to find it's no longer in the driveway! Is owning always the answer?

Sometimes an asset isn't an asset; it is actually a liability.

To many of us, homes may cost a substantial amount of money and you have to tie up some of your capital to start with (down payments). In our case, there's the lawn care people to pay, the pool people, and the air conditioning and heating systems that need cleaning and maintenance. There is always something breaking. For many people, it makes more sense to rent unless you have a ton of passive cash flow to pay for all the many things needed to keep the house in tip-top shape and to pay the mortgage. Now, if you have enough passive income to do this already (we are blessed to be at this point now), then this is a moot point. But if you don't, this matters. I wish we knew this stuff 20 years ago! Bigger is not better. More doesn't show your peers you are better. Get a handle on your finances. That is sexy! There is no shame in renting. A house is a liability. It costs you money; it doesn't make you money. Take the extra trapped capital and invest it to work for you. Retire sooner! In the long run, it might be cheaper to rent—and it also affords you the flexibility to move and you don't have to pay taxes, repairs, and insurances. You can live on the ocean, have a pool boy, and a restaurant downstairs... it doesn't have to be what you're thinking. It's an adage; it is definitely a mindset thing.

> *Sometimes an asset isn't an asset; it is actually a liability.*

For some people, it's smarter to lease their car. Cars are in constant need of care. Most leases can have a lower monthly fee and the dealer handles the maintenance. Heck, they even wash it and vacuum it out for you before you pick it up and have a killer coffee bar and lounge to sit in while you wait for it to be done. A leased car can be a company write off too. Just be smart about where you use your hard-earned cash.

> *Bigger is not better. More doesn't show your peers you are better. Get a handle on your finances. That is sexy!*

We are told to save our whole life too. The thing is, you make very little in interest with even the most aggressive savings plans (we get about 5.25 percent APY currently), so your money won't be making money that way for the long-term. If you have a 401K like many people do, it can fluctuate with the economy and you can lose out. Self-direct your IRAs and your 401K into cash flowing real estate. It's been a game changer for our wealth.

It might seem scary to take money out of your 401K or IRA, but it can do you a lot more good in a self-directed fund. With using places like RocketDollar or Quest as a custodian, you can self-direct that SDIRA into real estate! It will give you better returns and is backed by brick and mortar and land (real estate) instead of the market. Investing in the market is great... when it's great. But it's not always great, and it's scary. I am not a fan of the market. If you invest in high-risk stocks, you can win big or lose everything. If you invest in low-risk stocks, it might be safer, but no guts, no glory. It's a gamble no matter what. No one has control over the market. If you like it, put a bit in there but expand your portfolio to include real estate.

My mentor, Grant Cardone, says own 5 percent of 50 businesses rather than 100 percent of one. Fractional ownership can be a great way to build wealth and add to your legacy. This is how the sharks on *Shark Tank* do what they do. They own a ton of businesses but just a small part of each. They trade their expertise, experience, and contacts with the business owners for a percentage/piece of their business. Brilliant.

Interested in investing or acquiring an existing business? The process is very different from starting your own business. Here's a general outline:

1. Find the right opportunity. What kind of business are you looking to invest in? What industry do you have expertise in?

2. Market exploration: Check out and contact brokers, biz buy sell, online listings daily to see what's available

---

in your industry and in the location you're looking for (this takes the most time).

3. Submit an NDA/LOI. Determine stock or asset sale (We only do asset sales).

4. Due diligence: Once you've found something that fits your avatar, you will need to dissect and analyze the business' financials (p/l's, income statements, cash flow records), operations (understanding the day to day business), customer base, employees (analyze the workforce, skills, pay, vacation, benefits), legal standings (contracts, licenses/permits, litigations pending) and the works (this can also be a whole other book)!

5. Negotiate the deal (work out the purchase price, payment terms, contingencies). Seek advice from a business strategist, CPA, and your legal team.

6. Secure financing (conventional, SBA, seller financing)

7. Closing day and transition period (transfer of ownership and funds). Lawyer will orchestrate this with your accountant.

8. Execute 90 day post close—new owner on-site plan (strategy/plan to transition to your ownership and brand expectation)

When it comes to both your business and personal life, think before you buy. Is that purchase a smart investment or simply a waste of your hard-earned money? As *Rich Dad, Poor Dad* author Robert Kiyosaki says, "Rich people acquire assets. The poor and middle class acquire liabilities that they think are assets."

ACTION ITEMS:

- ☐ Buy assets, not liabilities (what can you sell or get rid of that you don't need).

- ☐ Seek out business opportunities and partnerships using the *Shark Tank* model. Exchange your expertise for a percentage in a business.

- ☐ Solidify two fractional businesses that you can become partners in. When you identify those two businesses, invest in ones that might bring you extra income.

- ☐ Compare the benefits from buying a home to renting one.

- ☐ If you like fancy cars and long for the latest models, consider leasing one so that your payments only go toward the time you lease it.

CHAPTER 10

SCALE YOUR BUSINESS

So many experts talk about the importance of growing your business to achieve and sustain success. Scaling is different. It's like multiplying your company's growth by 100!

Scaling was always the plan for me. I am not a simple person! I am driven and luckily, my partner in crime was and still is always behind me in the things I do, the dreams I have, and the plans for our future. We had a lot of decisions to make as we moved forward. We talked things out as they came up and decided our best plans as a team. Having the right partner and a team that has your back is imperative to be able to grow and scale your business. That team starts at the top. As an example, here's how we grew from one school to ultimately 20.

We started out in Canada, as you know. In the beginning, we would start one school at a time organically. When we saw that people from Windsor would drive to Lasalle, and folks from Lakeshore were willing to drive 30 minutes the wrong way to us on the other side of town to enroll their kids with us, we thought, let's just open a school for these folks in their communities (offering value). I wanted to grow each school organically and each school we opened were really big schools with lots of kiddos. That meant it took lots of time and training to open each site. There was no existing staff. We had to hire and train each person on the team. There were great advantages to this. We taught our systems, procedures, and culture from the jump. When you build and scale organically, you can build "little yous." Everyone learns to do things your way. You create the vibe and manage things the way you want. The drawback is that this way to scale is slow and calculated, and you have to be knee-deep in it all the way. We built our first three schools that way and I am still so proud of those builds and all those people.

We realized that the quicker way to scale was through acquisition. When we bought existing schools, it was a much faster process, but we also bought all the problems that came with the schools; everyone's so-called "baggage and bad habits." There were culture issues, substandard staff, and in fact, sometimes the parents and the students were just as challenging. We bought one set of schools that was essentially two locations. The owner was a Montessori-trained teacher, and at her location, things were run well. At their other location, things were pretty much a mess. We came in and needed to clean house. They called me the tsunami! I cleared out lots of staff for starters. The school was set up for 150 students. They had about 50 when I got there. I fired parents and 30 of the 50 kids. Basically, I started from scratch. My reputation, brand, and promise of excellence always came first. I never compromised quality for money or growth. It just wasn't in me and I still, to this day, feel the same about anything we do.

With the first set of Canadian schools, it took us about 10 years to acquire and build them. It was very slow and calculated. We did so through a lot of trial and error. No mentors; we learned lessons the hard way. We were also learning how to lead others, which is a challenge and a topic for an entirely other book or course.

From the first platform in 2001, we built those schools and ultimately sold all of them in 2011 to an international private equity group. We were approached by a private equity firm and though I didn't want to sell "my babies" (I called the schools my babies), they made an offer we simply couldn't refuse. We kept the buildings on some of the first schools we sold, and eventually we sold those to a real estate investor. This began to pique our interest in owning cash flowing properties when we saw the potential of passive income and what that could mean for us and our family.

We did a few other businesses in between, but my passion for preschools never waned and then we found ourselves back in the market, searching for some preschools for sale across the border in the USA, since my non-compete in Canada was vast. We bought the preschools in Omaha (I commuted weekly for 18 months), then later retired my husband from his successful mental health practice, moved our whole family to Omaha, and we started all over again. This time, we began by acquisition. Well, that was certainly a different beast, that's for sure. My plan was once again a ten-year one. I thought I would build to another 10 schools over a ten-year period and then look to sell them (by then I'd be 55 years old; sounded doable.) We acquired the nine schools in less than three years and started building the tenth location amidst the exciting times of the

Covid era, and then once again were approached by a private equity firm with a really fantastic offer. I really didn't want to sell this time. It was way too soon. I wasn't ready! I wasn't done! Things were happening really fast. But Beau said, "Can we really turn down this opportunity? Let's at least consider what they have to say."

As soon as you platform any business and your EBITDA—short for **E**arnings **B**efore **I**nterest, **T**axes, **D**epreciation, and **A**mortization, a metric that's used to evaluate the operating performance of a company—is over one million, you're going to get offers to sell. Truth is, that's the dream—to set yourself up for a private equity buy.

So, what I expected to take ten years happened in three and now we are here in Omaha. It's taken the kids and us a great deal of adjustment to find our space here. It takes time to make friends and learn to navigate a new country. We've learned a lot, and now we focus on helping folks in business do the same. You have to roll with the punches when you're in business.

ALERT: BRAGGING RIGHTS!!

READ THIS IF YOU ARE THINKING ABOUT SELLING YOUR BUSINESS OR HAVE OFFERS:

I recently worked with a client who had offers to buy her school. She was not looking at some simple things that would change the bottom line income for the buyers. They were offering two million, but she was incorrect in what their monthly/yearly income would be because there were things she was not taking into consideration.

After re-looking at all of her financial statements over the past several years, she was able to go back to the buyers with a new total expected income, and she got them to up the offer to over 3.5 million. This is what I love to do and why I do what I do for people who work with me.

As soon as we could, we bought a building for the school. We learned that the smartest thing to do was a sale-and-leaseback. What the heck is that? A sale-leaseback, or simply a leaseback, is a financial transaction where the owner of an asset, in this case our building, sells it and then leases it back from the new owner. However, in our case, we were the new owners of the building and became both the landlord and the tenant. We leased the building to our own school and eventually, many more of our schools. We set up a holding company to manage our real estate purchases. We became our own property management company and bought our building, then later all of our other buildings, and then leased the properties right back to us (through our other company). We paid our holding company (still us) the rent.

On top of this, we got a management fee to manage the properties. We were also owner-occupied, which helped us save on taxes and made it much more advantageous as we scaled to secure financing from lending institutions. We added schools one at a time at first, and over the years, we grew exponentially.

The other advantage of owning the buildings was that this was a fail-safe strategy. What if something happened, and we lost the schools? We could sell the real estate.

What if, God forbid, something had happened to either Beau or me? Who would handle the day to day of running multiple schools? By owning the buildings, we had a lucrative set of assets. The schools were set up with lots of smaller rooms. They didn't have to house schools. They could be business centers, medical offices, med-spas, or any number of things. Selling them without the schools was always a possibility.

And basically, that came to fruition. Eventually, we had scaled the schools to a platform of amazing locations and we were presented with an offer we couldn't refuse. We sold the schools to a private equity company. Our first transaction was not as smart as the latter (we sold to PE twice). We didn't have the advice of... well, frankly, someone like we are now. But we learned.

We came to understand that the most lucrative and smartest way to sell off all the rest of the schools was to sell the operations to one buyer. We sold the schools to private equity, coupled with a congruent sale of the real estate to a REIT—real estate investment trust. We had tenants who were high-level corporate entities. Like the tenants we have in our triple net deals, these were safe bets and provided us with a higher multiple on sale.

> *To scale, you will need to remove yourself to some degree and trust other people. You can't do everything.*

To get to all of this, there were concrete steps that had to be taken. These steps are pretty much the same, no matter what kind of business you plan to scale.

Let's look at those.

UNLOCKING GROWTH: THE ART AND SCIENCE OF SCALING

1. Step One: Building Excellence: The imperative of great people!

Your team is the thing that will make or break you. You need to recruit rock stars to work for and with you. You especially need a rock star team on your front line. Yes, Beau and I are a rock star team. I will say that without qualms, but even so, that was not enough for us to scale and even if you have a great partner or partners, you need amazing people. Whoever you ask to be the front-facing team member who will be interacting with your clients/customer base initially has to be solid and they need to be exceptional. You need to find and hire people who are already exceptional and who get your vision, want to share in your success, and even raise the bar with and for you, and then... train the hell out of them.

I am not going to lie. This is one of the hardest things, but remember what we talked about in the last chapter—being exceptional to start with. It's a lot easier to get rock stars to want to work with you when your reputation precedes you. No one wants to join a failing team. Successful people want to join and elevate successful teams.

You need to create a great interview process, be diligent about getting references, create a set of questions that get to the heart of what your business is about, and ask potential hires all of those questions. It's part of the systems and processes you need to create. Hiring is a process too. You must PAY to play!!! These folks don't come cheap. Hire them and then don't give them a salary ceiling! Give them the base pay only and let them soar! Let their innovation be the guide to how much money they can make themselves!

2. Unlock your Full Potential: Maximize EVERYTHING

Focus and be committed to maximizing your potential in every area of business. This is a huge part of scaling. Start by doing all the extra things we talked about in an earlier chapter. Create those added services you can offer to both new and especially existing clients to maximize value and profit. Create extra value and that will increase revenue—maximize that ebitda (earnings before interest, taxes, depreciation, and amortization). By offering all those additional services, it will mean more income that's generated per client, increasing your LCV (lifetime customer value). We talked a lot about this already, but you get the point. Give them more value, make more money for the company, pay your people more, quality gets better... and MAXIMIZE it all. It's cyclical.

Maximize your reach in the community. Become part of everything you can and show that you're more than just a business, you're a community advocate and partner.

Maximize your networking and marketing. Get known for maximum excellence of service and talent. Just go and MAX it out.

3. Crafting Excellence: Building Exceptional Systems

Systems are everything. The more you have and the tighter they are, the more your company will succeed and be poised for scaling and exit. First, you have to create them and then be diligent about implementing them. I was obsessed with having an exceptional set of processes and procedures. I realized that having Standard Operating Procedures (SOPs) and a detailed operational manual meant I would be able to scale it.

Building all those things, policies and procedures for staff, students, parents, day-to-day operations, safety and security, and rules for hiring and firing, takes time. You can't scale without creating unnecessary problems and pain without having the right systems in place. There are numerous automated systems to help with this nowadays, and no real excuses for not doing it. No systems, no sales. Companies are looking to purchase businesses with systems in place and that are running independent of you.

If you are thinking of ever selling your business and you are the business... you'd better know that isn't going to happen. The business has to run without you, and the only way for that to happen is by having the right people, the right SOPs, and the proper checks/balances in place.

To this end, you also need to understand and use the available technology so you can see all the things you need to see. Strategizing, planning, learning, evaluating, securing sales and revenue are all part of the SOP. It is important to make investments in technology. You need automation when scaling, even if you don't think you do or have some mental aversion to it. I admit to having that problem at first. When we moved to the United States and started buying schools here, we scaled the schools without using a CRM (customer relation management system). I thought, "We don't need that, we know how to do that shit." Yup, I was that cocky. We'd done it in Canada and didn't need that sort of system. Guess what? I was way wrong!

Implementing the CRM we were introduced to took us from 300 kids to 1200. It was 100 percent why we became more effective. With the CRM in place, I could read the KPIs I had created. Seeing those key indicators play out in a simple system allowed me to grow far more quickly. I could see things like how many people were coming through the door, how many were enrolling, who was closing sales, and how they were closing sales. I could find out exactly how long it took to complete the enrollment of a student or family and how many contacts/touches it took on average. I learned what we were doing wrong and what we were doing right. The average number of touches to close sales is seven times and really that goes for any kind of sale. If someone called our phone, we would say hello so-and-so and from there we would go into a very scripted conversation. When we joined a group for schools like ours (CCSA), we learned about the CRM they used and that was what we used for the entire time we owned the schools here in the states.

Back to the rock star concept, we hired a great enrollment specialist who was phenomenal!! She is family to us now.

She had an enrollment closing of 98 percent. She did tours, had great follow up, put them into the CRM, made sure they were set up for marketing automation and drip campaigns. I even had a hiring system in the CRM. I created funnels from LinkedIn and Indeed that allowed me to recruit the best possible team members.

4. Mastering the art of modern marketing: Developing your value proposition

Beyond those three steps, having a strong *marketing plan* is key to scaling. Once you market the first business, in our case a school, you learn what works and what doesn't. With marketing, you will likely need to be flexible. The demographics of one area may not be the same as in other areas. This is why businesses like Starbucks do intensive demographics studies before choosing locations. It's easier to find the location where the demographics meet their marketing than trying to adapt their highly branded marketing to other areas. Also, they know what demographics mean success. Location, location, location.

If you have a strong brand, a reputation for excellence, a rock star team, your systems are in place (yes, your staff and systems are part of your brand too), and referrals being offered regularly, minor adjustments in your marketing won't be too difficult. Like Starbucks, when we scaled, we looked at places where students were coming from and knew that if we had parents willing to travel to enroll their students in our school—because we were worth it—we could open a school in that location and those parents would help drive others to us. The demographics bore out that outcome. It may not be that simple for your business. Another reason to belong to peer networking groups, masterminds, and... GET A MENTOR.

All these things are how you scale. People are number one in our business. We knew we had to focus on what we could do for more people if we had more schools. Following the steps, creating the right systems, getting excited about technology and using it to help automate everything, getting your marketing right. We also used a marketing company, Grow Your Center (GYC), for this and it was a game changer for us to have the right tools in place, learning to embrace and utilize social media are all the stages that enable you to support the growth, including within your own company. To scale, you will need to remove yourself to some degree and trust other people. You can't do everything. You're going to need IT support, budgeting tools, and the support of your team and the people you network with and are mentored by.

But only you can decide how far you want to take your business and then commit to grow to the level you want. The truth is, the sky is the limit.

ACTION ITEMS:

☐ Understand the difference between growth and scaling. Are you ready to scale your business, with all the commitment it entails?

☐ Research CRMs. Do a trial with one or two that look good to you.

☐ Create a great hiring funnel. Encourage innovation and idea shares from your team.

☐ Create SOPs and a solid foundation of principles you will not waiver on.

☐ Create best practices. Then, abide by and follow your best practices.

☐ Hire a marketing agency (vet them; they aren't all good).

☐ Use technology wherever you can.

☐ Google networking groups that are more specific to your business model and ones that have people who might be farther along the road than you are.

CHAPTER 11

CULTIVATE CONNECTIONS

I realized early on that I could not do everything without some expert help. When we moved to the United States from Canada, the learning curve was totally different. I needed mentorship. At first, that meant joining group mentoring programs. I wasn't completely new to the concept of mentoring help. I belonged to a business accelerator in Windsor that was free. But in a new country, starting schools with a new set of rules, I needed to get more advice and build more community.

I went to a conference and heard what the speaker/owner (Kris Murray) had to say, and I thought, yeah, this is exactly what I need. So, when she pitched her year-long program, I ponied up the money, not a trivial amount, and joined the highest level she offered (Empire) in the Childcare Success Academy. What I paid to join that program paid for itself a hundred times over in value by being part of that group. It accelerated my learning curve and helped me avoid the kind of pitfalls that I'd fallen into in the past. The leader of the group and many of my fellow members were experts who had learned a ton from their mistakes and successes, for that matter. The whole idea of a group mentoring program is to be in the room with peers and with someone leading the group who knows more than the members. If you're the smartest person in the room, that's the wrong room.

Getting mentorship gave me practical and real-life knowledge and advice. The people in the group had real world experience, and they were living the same life I was. I had the ability to talk to a mentor and other people who had been there and done that. I was in a new country with new rules and I was hiring people whose culture was a bit different than mine. You might think that Canada and America are similar countries. We share a border and have similarities for sure, but at the same time, we are very different in our approach to things, especially education. I had new issues with employees, procedures, processes, and many things that happened to us in the acquisition process. I was able to save a lot of time and headaches and compress timelines by asking advice from people who had the real world know-how.

After we sold, I realized that while the group setting for mentoring was incredibly valuable for childcare, in order for me to go faster (and by now you know me well enough to know that faster is my speed) in this new REI industry (I had to learn quickly how to eradicate a large passive income tax bill), I had to get 1:1 personal mentorship. I needed to really compress the timelines and focus on fast and effective. It was time to look for the right one-on-one mentorship program. I have worked with a couple of high-level coaches and what we were able to get to was to say, "Here are the issues. Here's how we work through that. Here is my specific situation." We then tailor the solutions to me and my unique issues. The mentors I worked with closely and still work with, help me determine what to do, issue by issue, and work through each one.

I've spent hundreds of thousands (yup, you read that right) on mentorship programs. Some great, some not so great. The ones I like best are the ones that provide me with measurable results. One of the best experiences I've had was my 1:1 mentoring with my coach, Grant Cardone. Working one-on-one with Grant was game changing for me. It's not so much that he solves problems for me, but it is more about how he moves my mindset. He has taught me to be constantly thinking bigger, and he has a way of giving it to me straight and real. He is no nonsense. I have big dreams. I want to keep growing and learning. I want to be in rooms where people are doing insane things!! Working with him helps me truly see that everything is indeed possible, and he is proof of how we can all get there. I have learned how to build the roadmap for my success by working backwards from my North Star. That way of thinking has helped me personally as well as professionally. I do that for everything now. I think in terms of what I want to do, and I create a plan based on my end goal in every aspect of my life. You need to set targets.

One of the biggest advantages in having a mentor that is in the hemisphere that you are aspiring to be in, is that it can get you entry into rooms with people at a completely different level. They are playing at a level you want to be at and stay at. I want to be where Grant Cardone and the people he associates with are. Personal mentoring cuts through the minutia and gets me into private groups, like the billionaire boardroom group that we are part of. Being in the room with these folks is beyond anything I've ever experienced. I've had dinner with Brandon and Natalie Dawson. I have had incredible conversations with folks that are leagues and billions above me. These meetings and conversations push me to grow, and to be committed to constantly do better.

> *People are either building your empire or tearing it down.*
>
> *- Elena Cardone*

As you scale, your mentorship needs to scale too. As you grow, you will grow out of some groups and into others. Start where you are, but like I said before, just START! Industry-specific cohorts support people in the same industry. That worked for us and it might work for you as a starting point. Working with and being mentored by people who have the same problems with staffing, systems, and more gave us a community that was supporting us.

> *Mentorship gives me perspective. Proximity is POWER.*

Another bonus is the confidence boost you get from mentoring. Entrepreneurship is a lonely road even when you have partners and family support. Having peers tell you, "You have this" is awesome. I hear that and think, *yeah, yeah, I do have this. I can do this*. My fellow group members, my mentors, and my peers show me that they believe in me. Even though you believe in yourself, and I do, having someone say, "You got this" really helps! The feedback I've received along the way on where to improve is another thing. I can't see myself. I don't have a magic mirror. Having a personal check-up on where I am at, what I am doing right and wrong makes a world of difference. I am the be all end all in my businesses, the boss, but who's checking on me? My mentors fill that role.

> *Another bonus is the confidence boost you get from mentoring. Entrepreneurship is a lonely road even when you have partners and family support. Having peers tell you, "You have this" is awesome.*

Mentorship gives me perspective. I have been in many different groups, with lots of people sharing diverse viewpoints. I got to see where I fit and learned things I wanted to adopt and reject. Learning from people who had tripped over their mistakes saved my ass more than a few times. I would think that I wanted to do something for my business (in my new country especially), only to find out that the concept might not work in my market. I could hear from people who had been there and done that, who could tell me what to keep, what to alter, what to tweak, and, in some instances, what to simply NOT do.

From those communities, I have built some true and lasting friendships. I have also met some folks I would rather not emulate. It is all great learning either way. I have gained emotional support integral to my and our company's growth. No matter what kind of business you have or are in, even solopreneurs, speakers, authors, and coaches, getting a mentor or being part of a mentoring cohort is going to be the game changer. Nothing else would have moved me that fast, especially in America. We scaled far more quickly by implementing the action items we were given, like adopting and embracing the CRM, which I would never have done.

Go to conferences. Meet new people. Get advice on how to grow and scale. Hire people for things you're not good at. Get the who's you need, don't worry about the how! At the end of the day, all issues are rooted in only three things: people, processes, and revenue. Your issues are financial, staff, or systems. Share those problems with folks in a business mastermind with people who can help. Don't be too proud or shy to get help and, for goodness sake, don't believe that you already know everything. I promise... YOU DON'T!

Which brings me to the concept of networking. I network constantly. At this point in my career, that means a very different level of networking than when I started, but the thing is to START! Start where you are. I don't mean location so much as business level. If you do a lot of local business, you might want to join the chamber of commerce in your town or other local networking groups that meet in person. There are a lot of women-centric groups, ladies—Google them and ask other women business owners what groups they belong to. There are so many networking groups in the world. For us, a game changer was joining one specific to our industry. If you're a speaker, coach or consultant who needs to get on stages or create workshops, there are groups specific to sharing info with other speakers. There are free groups you can join if you can't afford a paid group, but word of warning, they are often not as powerful as groups that cost something to attend. BNI (Business Networking International) will cost you to join but many people swear by them, especially service-based businesses like landscapers, plumbers, and building contractors. BNI is an "industry specific" group, meaning only one plumber, one web designer, etc. They are not for everyone because it's a freaking commitment. Weekly meetings must be attended and there's lots of pressure to send referrals to one another. If you're into strict rules, they might be for you.

There are also plenty of networking groups that meet only online. Covid made some of these groups pop up and grow even stronger. Find the ones that work for you. Show up to meetings and share who you are and what you do. Connect with people who can help you and where you can also help others. Sometimes it's just good to know that you are not alone, that your problems are not all that unique, and to have people who have been where you are and can advise you. You might find a mentor and even become a mentor. We will talk about the power of mentorship in one of the next chapters. The point is, get out there in those "communities." Communities can be created anywhere, not just on Main Street. Find your tribes and become the exceptional business of note. Not only will you make business friends, get great advice as well as give it, but once you get established with the networking groups that make the most sense for you, you will have an outside sales force of people who like you, trust you, and will send warm, even hot, leads to you.

An important thing to note, though: If you are the smartest, most successful person in the room, whether it's a networking group, a mastermind, or conference, YOU ARE IN THE WRONG ROOM! I don't ever want to be the smartest person in groups I belong to or pay for coaching and mentorship with anyone unless they know stuff I don't know. I want to learn and grow, not just be the know-it-all. If I'm not learning, I'm out. I am seeking the next best group, people, and level for me.

Remember that if you are not learning, or you are always being the one offering the advice in a group or mastermind, it may be time to jump out. There are groups I will always belong to and not all of them are super expensive. I have belonged to the Entrepreneurs Organization—EO— and that costs me $6000 a year ($500 a month). One of the biggest reasons that organization is so valuable is that it's an international organization. There are trips I can go on, zooms with companies all over the world, and there is so much education I can take part in and learn from, including a lot of info on AI right now. It has always been enough for me to stay in the group. You don't outgrow global platforms and this one is affordable.

The big takeaway is to find your mentors. Look for ones where you are not the smartest or most successful person in the room. Reach up. Grow in and out of groups and into one-on-one mentors. The main thing is to get started.

HOW TO CHOOSE THE RIGHT MENTOR—10 KEY CONSIDERATIONS:

1. **Alignment.** Do they align with your goals/ethics? Are y'all on the same page?

2. **Expertise and Experience.** Have they done what you want to do?

3. **Track Record of Success.** Have they successfully mentored others? How many times?

4. **Communication Style.** Can they provide constructive feedback? Can they explain concepts in the way you require?

5. **Accessibility and Commitment.** Do they have the time for you?

6. **Compatibility.** Do your personalities and working styles mesh?

7. **Willingness and Enthusiasm.** Are they excited to mentor you?

8. **Networking Opportunities.** Do they have a "Rolodex" of folks they can introduce you to?

9. **Personal Development.** Will they invest in your personal growth?

10. **Cost and Compensation.** Do they fit the bill... literally?

ACTION ITEMS:

☐ Get networking! Find your tribe. Don't be afraid to pay for them... quality is key here.

☐ Look into masterminds or mentoring groups, both on-line and in person.

☐ Research mentors and make a plan to grow toward someone you admire and can learn from.

☐ Evaluate what masterminds you are in, what they are giving you, and whether you are still growing in them.

☐ Who is in your "reference group"? Remember that dictates 99 percent of your success.

☐ Proximity is Power. Never underestimate paying for high-level coaching that works.

☐ Don't say you can't afford mentorship, or you can't afford not to have a mentor. Figure out a plan of how to increase income to afford the right mentor for you.

☐ See where your ideal clients are hanging out, what services they are using etc., and partner and sponsor those events and services. Commit to two sponsorships today.

CHAPTER 12

SAVE MONEY ON TAXES

I n this chapter, I'm going to tell you what you need to know about taxes to keep the most money in your pocket—lawfully. There is nothing in this book that I'm not currently using or haven't previously used or tried before. I am all about saving you time and avoiding costly mistakes.

Disclaimer: I'm not a CPA and this stuff may be boring!

This entire chapter might be boring to you, but it's actually very useful information. Get your Starbucks if you want to read it or use this section to make yourself sleepy before bed.

If you hate talking about taxes and can't make it through this, forward it to your CPA or bookkeeper. If you know all of this, just skip it.

> *The tax code is a huge book. The first three pages tell you how to pay tax and how much, and the other 50 tell you how not to pay tax!!*

If you're a new or aspiring entrepreneur, there are legal tax strategies you might not be familiar with but NEED to know about.

I mentioned that we hired our kids using the $13,000 a year allotment. Yes, it's great for them and their path to financial literacy, but it is also a tax break for us. We get to claim that $13,000 times four kids on our tax return. (That's a nice $52k) and they get to realize that work produces a nice monetary outcome!

But there are several other legal tax strategies that can save you a lot of money when filing your business taxes. Like sooo many more! The tax code is a huge book. The first three pages tell you how to pay tax and how much, and the other 50 tell you how not to pay tax!! Most of us only understand or even look at the first three pages. Here's one that you may not know about. A vehicle over 6,000 pounds can be considered a commercial vehicle like a truck. This includes luxury SUVs like a Range Rover, GWagon (which I bought under this rule) or Escalade—many of which are over that weight limit. The Automobile Tax Deduction Rule—Section 179—allows you to write-off 100 percent of the vehicle's depreciation in year one if the vehicle is used 100 percent for business and you buy it brand new from a dealership. You can't buy the SUV from a neighbor, your brother, or Facebook Marketplace. There are some rules you will want to talk over with your tax accountants, but this is just an example of one of the many.

Have you ever heard of the Augusta rule?

The Augusta Rule began when residents/homeowners of Augusta, Georgia, started renting out their homes during the annual Masters Tournament. The rule was meant for personal use, but business owners can use this for a tax break too. You can rent the house you live in tax-free for 14 days or less in any given year.

There are the requirements you have to meet to do this, though, and keep meticulous records.

1. The rent amount can't be way more than the going rate and must be in line with similar rentals. You can do a Google search and get comps.

2. The property must be in the U.S. It doesn't have to be your primary residence, but we're not talking about your condo in Costa Rica here.

3. The total days rented for the year must be 14 days or less for each property you own.

4. You have to keep copious records and document the rent payment. If you're renting to your own business, have a formal rental agreement in place and issue a 1099-MISC to your business for the amount paid.

5. You have to claim the rent income on your personal tax return and then exclude it under IRS Section 280A (the Augusta Rule).

Besides sticking to the rules and documenting the payments, you will need to be able to substantiate the business activity during the rental days. This means documenting the meeting agenda, minutes, a list of the people who attended and, to be safe, take pictures. The more the better to avoid an audit. If you also get paid rent for your home office or your home is your primary place of business, you'll likely violate the Augusta rule.

For example: Do you have professional development, team meetings, strategy sessions, or wknd retreats? If so, have them at your home... deduct the number of days you use per year (up to 14) using this rule.

It's a little complicated, but once you set this up for the first year, you will be able to replicate it year after year.

The Safe Harbor Election is another tax break we implement. This one is a little complicated but I will give you the 50-foot view so you can bring it up with your tax accountant. Basically, it goes like this: when you purchase items for your business, you can either deduct the full cost of the expense at once, or you can deduct the cost over multiple years (depreciation). You do better to do one-time expenses and will get a bigger refund if you take the deduction in one year rather than depreciating an asset over multiple years.

The Safe Harbor Election lets you deduct the full cost of items worth $2,500 or less, instead of spreading out the depreciation. You can also potentially use it to expense the cost of improvements to your business buildings if you qualify. But like I said, this one is best to give to your tax accountant.

Income tax is paid on earnings from employment, interest, dividends, royalties, or self-employment, whether it's in the form of services, money, or property.

Capital gains tax is paid on income that derives from the sale or exchange of an asset, such as a stock or property that's categorized as a capital asset.

KEY FACTS

- The U.S. income tax system is progressive, with rates ranging from 10 percent to 37 percent of a filer's yearly income. Rates rise as income rises.
- For tax purposes, short-term capital gains are treated as ordinary income on assets held for one year or less.
- Long-term capital gains are given preferential tax rates of 0 percent, 15 percent, or 20 percent, depending on your income level.
- Long-term capital gains taxes apply to assets held for over a year when sold.
- Income and capital gains tax brackets are adjusted annually for inflation.

The IRS considers taxable income by separating income into two main categories: "ordinary income" and "realized capital gain." Ordinary income includes your earned wages, any income from rentals, and income from the interest you gain in the tax year on loans, CDs, and bonds (except for municipal bonds). Capital gain is the money you make in a tax year from the sale of a capital asset (stock, real estate, etc). This means the property sold at a price higher than you paid for it. The difference is taxable.

Super important fact: If your asset goes up in price but you **do not sell it**, you have not realized your capital gain and therefore **owe no tax**.

Note that long-term realized capital gains are subject to a substantially lower tax rate than ordinary income. So, investors have a big incentive to hold on to your appreciated assets for at least a year and a day. By doing this, the asset qualifies as long-term and is subject to the much lower rates.

These rates are 0 percent, 15 percent, or 20 percent, depending on your income level. In 2022, a single filer with an income of $41,675 or less paid 0 percent on long-term capital gains. If the person's income was over $41,675 up to $459,750, the rate went to 15 percent. It jumped up to 20 percent, if income was over $459,750.

For 2023, the thresholds were slightly higher: you paid 0 percent on long-term capital gains if you had an income of $44,625 or less; 15 percent if you had an income of over $44,625 up to $492,300; and 20 percent if your income exceeded $492,300.

ACTION ITEMS:

☐ Read the first three pages of the Tax Code, which tell you how to pay taxes and how much.

☐ Keep meticulous records of your business expenses because every penny counts and may impact how much tax you owe. (Or don't!)

☐ Familiarize yourself with the Augusta Rule if you plan on renting your house for a few weeks—tax free.

☐ Ask your accountant about the Safe Harbor Election, which lets you deduct the full cost of items worth $2,500 or less, instead of spreading out the depreciation.

☐ Learn about Bonus Depreciation and Cost Segregation.

☐ Invest in real assets.

CHAPTER 13

PUT YOUR FAMILY'S TRUST IN TRUSTS

A s a mom, I want to leave my children a legacy, both personal and financial. So, let's talk about generational wealth—ensuring that the bucks don't stop when you do! Trusts help your loved ones avoid probate and protect your legacy. There are many benefits of setting up a trust, and you don't have to be rich to do this. I realize that our old money mindset makes this seem scary to many people. No one wants to think about dying, but it's a reality.

What exactly is a trust?

From Dummies.com—trust for dummies—This is a simple way to look at trusts:

A trust agreement is a document that spells out the rules that you want to be followed for property held in trust for your beneficiaries. Common objectives for trusts are to reduce the estate tax liability, protect property in your estate, and avoid probate.

Check out the book if this subject interests you.

THERE ARE SOME VERY IMPORTANT BASICS TO KNOW BEFORE YOU GET STARTED ON CREATING A TRUST.

- There has to be a person in charge—usually called the trustor, settlor, or grantor. That's **you**. You're the one "granting" the assets to someone or some entity.

- There has to be a trustee. You need to know who that will be and it should be someone you... trust! They need to know all the rules, be willing to manage the trust, and make sure things are always kept in order.

- What kind of trust is best? There are different kinds of trusts. A trust can have one goal, like how your money is distributed to your two children, or it can have multiple objectives or goals. Once you decide on the type of trust you're setting up, you need to know and follow the rules of that type of trust.

- If you put property in trust, that is now considered "trust property."

- Who are the beneficiaries of the trust? This can be a person, several people, or an institution like a school, a charity, or a non-profit. These people will be getting your property/money at some point.

There are two main types of trusts—revocable or irrevocable. Revocable means you can "revoke" or cancel it. So basically, irrevocable means: no can do. They cannot be changed once you create them.

As long as you're still living, a revocable trust is *you*, and you can change things and even cancel it. Revocable trusts are containers that hold all your business and even personal assets, including your personal residence. Any asset with your personal name attached goes into your revocable trust. Revocable trusts are flow-through entities, meaning that the trust doesn't file its own tax return. Instead, trust activities show up on the personal tax return of the grantor... again, that's you!

Irrevocable trusts can't be changed once they've been created. The assets held can't be removed or canceled. Irrevocable trusts can be used to remove certain assets from your control and separate those assets from your business assets. They also file their own tax returns separate from the grantor and they come with their own tax rate. That rate could be much higher than your personal tax rate. Again, this is why you need to have a good tax accountant or someone that can advise you on how to set these things up, so you're making decisions that give you the best tax advantages.

A living trust is a kind of revocable trust. These trusts are *living* entities, meaning they're revocable for as long as the grantor is still living. Once the grantor dies, the trust becomes irrevocable. They help with estate planning and protecting your assets.

These are different from wills. Living trusts offer more benefits than simply writing a will, the biggest being that your beneficiaries can avoid probate with a Living Trust. Wills are just instructions on what to do with your assets once you pass on. That list must go through probate before a judge via probate and the judge determines where the assets go. Probate invites the opportunity for people to contest the will. This takes time and costs money, which comes out of the estate assets. All kinds of crazy things can happen when a will goes through probate.

Living trusts don't have to go through the court system after you die. While you're alive, your living trust basically owns your personal assets so, when you die, all the decisions have been laid out and the courts don't have any reason to get involved. Your assets are held in the name of the trust and get distributed the way you set things up for the trustee you left in charge. Living trusts can cost a little more to set up, but they're way less expensive compared to what it will cost your estate if your will goes into probate.

There are many kinds of trusts, including land trusts and personal property trusts. Land trusts are what they sound like, to hold land/real estate property. Personal property trusts are for pretty much anything other than land/real estate. Could be your interest in a business partnership or your car even. The main thing to get from all of this is to look into trusts and determine what's best for you and your family. You will need to get help with this from an attorney to make sure you choose wisely and set things up in the best way possible for your beneficiaries. Ours are a little complicated, but we want to be sure that the legacy we've built lives on long after we are potting soil.

ACTION ITEMS:

☐ Define your trust objectives—asset protection, estate planning? What is the goal of the trust?

☐ Choose the right type of trust.

☐ Select trustee and beneficiaries.

☐ Make sure you have detailed information about what goes in the trust—consult with your CPA on the financial part.

☐ Draft the trust with your estate planning lawyer.

☐ Fund the trust.

☐ Provide guidance on the management of the trust and educate your beneficiaries.

CHAPTER 14

INVEST IN REAL ESTATE TO CREATE PASSIVE INCOME

As you know, we initially built wealth at our Montessori schools through hard work, calculated risk, a commitment to providing an exceptional customer experience, and gradually growing and expanding our business. We sold the first set of schools in Canada and that journey stretched over a 10-year period. But when we got to America, we reached ownership of 10 new schools in the United States much more quickly. The way we did this was to acquire groups of schools instead of growing organically. We were actively marketing, building, and scaling our business. Suddenly, we had a lucrative buyout offer from a private equity company. We realized we could move away from active, earned income and into passive, generational wealth, building through real estate investments. And that's what Beau and I do now—investing in real estate and coaching others on how to replicate our success for themselves.

Our model is to buy cash-producing assets only. This is why we invest in triple net, multi-family and storage/industrial real estate and why we offer this kind of investment to our client partners. These are assets that produce income and increase in value over time and help us to eradicate tax and build legacy wealth as well. We want investments that offer recurring cash flow for income and appreciation for legacy wealth

But HOW?

Well… we were approached by a private equity firm after only three years instead of the 10 I had planned on. They presented us with an offer we couldn't refuse. So, after a grueling number of months, we took the offer!

Once the schools were in the process of being sold, we began to rethink not only our financial plan but our entire life plan. Up to that point, our income was earned. We worked our tails off for it. We had never realized there was a better way up until that point, and I can tell you—I wish we had known then what we know now. That is a lot of why I wrote this book. I want people to learn what we did and, if possible, sooner than we did.

We met with our advisors, did lots more research, and decided our best bet was to take the money from the sale of the school properties and begin reinvesting in different kinds of real estate. We coupled the sale of the schools (to a Private Equity— PE—company) and the sale of all the buildings (to a REIT), which housed all of the ten schools with a 15 year NNN lease in place with the new highly-rated tenancy.

In case that's Greek to you, a REIT (pronounced reet) is a kind of mutual fund. They basically buy real estate instead of putting their investors' hard earned money into stocks (we all know how that can go). They have a particular tax status based on the idea that they have to pay 90 percent of the profits they make on the real estate to their shareholders, which is referred to as dividends (like Monopoly!). So long as they do that, they don't get taxed like a regular corporation like other businesses.

So, we sold the buildings to one of these large REITS. But now, we had a big huge capital gain to deal with and that would mean HUGE tax! That would be a different story if we reinvested in other real estate. In America, there is something called the 1031 tax structure. If you take all the money you make in a real estate transaction and use those gains to buy other real estate, the tax on that gain is deferred. We sold our brick and mortar properties, flipped that equity into a 1031 by buying into different classes of NNN real estate. The triple net property creates monthly passive income (stable and consistent cash flow). There is zero landlord responsibility, and we are paid consistently through monthly rent. This replaced all and more of our active income.

The REIT bought all of the buildings together in one fell swoop. They gave us a higher multiple on that, based on the fact that we had triple net (NNN) and highly-rated corporate guaranteed tenants for 15 years in those buildings. We had a solid NNN in place because the people buying the schools paid monthly market rent (Always key to charge yourself market rent if you are ever planning to sell). Like any other triple net, they were responsible for everything, and there were fail safes in the way of predetermined rent bumps and guarantees built into the leases. This meant the value of the property was much higher to the REIT because of the guaranteed income with a highly-rated tenant locked into a very long and stable lease. We had made them sign a 15-year NNN lease for each school as part of the conditions of sale.

So, we began buying our own triple net properties (NNNs). We created a cash flow generator with predetermined, corporate tenants who paid their rent and provided us a consistent, stable, passive income. That was great, but now, because of all that passive income, we were looking at a huge tax bill at the end of the year.

> *Investment income will provide you the means to long-term wealth.*

Now what? We had to learn how to eradicate some of that tax burden. We met some people in one of our mentor networking groups who had advice on this and we hopped on a call. Once again, we spoke to our advisors, as well as our CPA, and our tax strategist. The answer was to get into buying multi-family properties to eradicate the income tax. The United States government offers bonus depreciation on certain things. One of the main areas they give tax bonuses on are housing, particularly apartments. The government has no interest in wanting to build or buy multi-family properties to become landlords. They want someone else to do that, namely investors like us. They also give bonuses on things like oil and gas, agriculture and farming, and a few other things. For us, we liked housing and apartment complexes as a place to invest.

We started out as an LP (Limited Partner) in these investments, but later realized it made more sense for us to be GPs (General Partners). We just had to learn the ropes. When buying these properties, we could use the entire bonus depreciation—100 percent of whatever the bonus depreciation was against our taxes in year one. In 2023, it is 80 percent. So, let's say we had a bonus depreciation of $100,000 on any property. We could take $80,000 off that amount as depreciation against our taxes!! In 2024 it's 60%! The debt market is different this year, so it has changed the amount of depreciation being offered. We will need to invest higher amounts as the depreciation amounts are lower, since the LTV (loan to value) is lower.

What we have arrived at is, what we call, the perfect triad of our wealth structure. Our triple net properties are pumping our cash flow from the rent (we live off this), the multi-family properties create the depreciation to eradicate the tax, and then we dabble in some storage and industrial as well (that offers a bit of both). These properties allow us to increase our personal net wealth, while adding to our legacy wealth structure for our kids and family. We live 100 percent off of our passive income while also enjoying a 100 percent tax free living. We built an income generator and a tax income "eraser."

Okay, Julie, that's great for you guys, but how do we start this?

To begin with, you have to have income from a W2 job or a business. You need to have an external amount of income to begin to invest in real estate, or anything for that matter. If you don't have disposable income, money you don't need to live on and pay your bills, you're not likely ready to invest in anything the way we do or the way we teach our clients, family, and friends to do. So, you must grow your investment income... or sell your business (have a large capital event).

Investment income will provide you the means to long-term wealth. It's the safest route to overall legacy wealth for your children and family.

Let's begin with NNNs. NNN is the acronym for a triple net lease. NNNs are agreements on a property where the tenant or lessee promises to pay rent and all utilities like most rentals. In addition, the tenant will pay all the expenses of the property, including real estate taxes, building insurance, and maintenance. NNN leases are available on commercial properties such as retail stores, office spaces, and even warehouses.

There are other types of standard commercial leases, where some or all of the aforementioned payments fall on the responsibility of the landlord. For example, a single net lease requires tenants to pay property taxes plus rent. A double net lease typically tacks on property insurance to that agreement in addition to the taxes. In both of these options, the landlord would be responsible for general repairs, maintenance, landscaping, snow removal (location dependent), or some variation thereof.

For our investment clients, we focus on investing in single tenant properties with NNN leases and corporate guarantees (the tenants are a corporation, and they guarantee the lease). These opportunities provide solid, stable, and consistent investment returns. In addition, a great benefit to this type of NNN lease is that it requires MINIMAL TO ZERO LANDLORD RESPONSIBILITIES!

Why should you consider investing in these properties? Let me tell you about the fantastic benefits they offer. We love them!!!

Here's why NNN investments stand out as a game-changer:

Security, Stability, and Predictability: NNN Corporate Guaranteed Properties provides an added layer of security. With a long-term lease in place (often 10-20 years), you can enjoy a predictable and steady income stream. Many times this can be the full 20 years. The goal is to hold these properties until the cap rate and rent bump come together to make the most for the investors. They are definitely longer-term investments. They cash flow for us on day 1! Sometimes the market shifts and a sale is possible earlier, as cap rate compressions can happen at any time.

Strong, Creditworthy Tenants: These properties are leased by (investment grade) reputable national or multi-national corporations, meaning you have a reliable tenant with a strong credit rating. You can rest assured that your investment is in safe hands! The added security of a corporate tenant guarantee means that even if the tenant faces challenges, the corporation steps in, safeguarding your rental income and providing peace of mind. With corporate-backed NNN investments, you have the opportunity to partner with high-quality tenants, such as established national or multi-national corporations. These tenants boast strong credit ratings and solid financial positions, reducing the likelihood of lease defaults and ensuring a reliable income source for your investment. We have even added a ROFR as an added layer of protection on our childcare properties!

What the heck is a ROFR?! It's a first right of refusal on the operations of the tenant's business so that in case anything were to ever happen in the future (they would have to close nationally), we can fully control the business operations!

On the NNN example described below and on other properties that are childcare-related, we negotiated into the lease a ROFR. Meaning, if the current lease owner wanted to sell that childcare business, we would have the right to purchase the business first. Allowing us to operate the childcare business while simultaneously being our own landlord. With 30-plus years of childcare experience under our belt, we understand this business model extremely well and so a ROFR made sense.

An example of one of our NNNs

We recently offered an NNN investment for syndication, where The Learning Experience (TLE), a national childcare company, was the tenant. These guys, of course, had a great credit rating. Childcare is an essential service even in a recession. Tuition rates were the highest in the Southlake area of Texas where the school was. These characteristics supported the fact that this was an amazing asset. This particular location was full with a waitlist for students, and the location is a corporate flagship site for training. It's decked out to the hills and when folks spend this type of money on TI's, they aren't going anywhere!!

Why invest in NNN's?

Potential for Appreciation: As the value of the property can appreciate over time, you have the potential to see your investment grow. Plus, if the property is well-located, it may attract more tenants in the future, further enhancing its value. This location had that in spades, making the investment even more of a no-brainer.

Passive Income: NNN properties are often considered a hands-off investment, as the tenant takes care of all of the expenses. This allows you to enjoy passive income without the hassle of day-to-day management. This hands-off approach frees up your time while still generating steady cash flow.

Inflation Hedge: NNN leases provide a stable income source that typically includes rent escalation clauses tied to inflation, providing a built-in hedge against rising prices. This can help protect the purchasing power of your investment over the long-term. We only buy new, off market properties that have rent bumps built into our leases. This particular one offered 10 percent increases at years 6, 11, and 16. Bonus!

Diversification: Investing in NNN Corporate Guaranteed Properties offers diversification beyond traditional stocks and bonds and outside of the multi-family scene. By including commercial real estate in your portfolio, you can spread your risk and potentially enhance your overall returns. The cash flow starts on day one, which means you're not waiting to see ROI. By incorporating commercial real estate into your holdings, you gain exposure to a resilient asset class that historically delivers favorable returns.

The syndication model enables you to participate in larger deals and access opportunities that were once out of reach. (Own less percent of each property but own more properties!!) This also helps mitigate risk, preserve capital, and build wealth.

Minimal Management Responsibilities: Unlike traditional real estate investments, NNN properties relieve you of the day-to-day management hassles. Your tenants handle property-related expenses, repairs, and maintenance, allowing you to focus on other ventures or enjoy passive income. A simple check-in is all that is required.

Diverse Tenant Base: NNN properties often attract reputable corporate tenants, such as national retailers, pharmacies, and well-established companies. These tenants usually have solid financial standing, reducing the risk of potential vacancies and ensuring consistent rental payments.

Potential for Capital Appreciation: Alongside the steady cash flow, NNN properties can appreciate in value over the long-term. Growing demand for such investments, increased NOI's through rent bumps, coupled with desirable locations and strong tenant relationships, can lead to attractive capital appreciation opportunities. As the real estate market evolves and demand increases, the underlying property's value can rise, offering you the potential for capital appreciation and long-term wealth accumulation.

Future-Proof Investment: NNN with corporate guarantees aligns well with long-term investment goals. The stability, reliable income, and strong tenant base provided by corporate-backed leases create a resilient investment model. This can help you weather economic fluctuations and provide a reliable income stream even during challenging times like today's markets.

To capitalize on this type of investment opportunity, it's essential to conduct thorough research, evaluate the tenant's creditworthiness, and select properties strategically. Working with us, we can help provide valuable insights and guidance throughout your investment process. This is why we do what we do. That's why we are involved in these so heavily. We've been investing in NNN properties for over 25 years, and we live exclusively off the income derived from them! We have a lot of our own money in each of our deals. We would not do these deals, nor would we share this kind of investment, if we truly didn't love and believe in it! We are a Boutique real estate investment group. We created this real estate investment business for us, our friends, family, and clients, originally as a spin-off of our active income business so that we could help solve the problem of creating generational wealth for us and our clients.

We believe in the personal touch. We offer consistent and transparent communication, and beautiful high-end, cash flowing properties in fantastic locations. We're super picky and we do only about four to six great deals a year. We believe in quality over quantity, 100 percent of the time.

NNN investments offer investors a unique avenue to generate consistent income while mitigating risks. But when combined with a corporate guarantee, the potential for financial success becomes even more compelling.

> ❝ *We've been investing in NNN properties for over 25 years, and we live exclusively off the income derived from them!*

With our Real Estate holding company, we do about four to six deals a year, which investors like you can join. We definitely consider ourselves a boutique real estate investment club. We have about 1,000 people or more in our Facebook community as well as an active email list of folks who avidly invest in our deals. These are our educational platforms. We go into the group and allow folks to come and learn at a base level what we are doing. They can ask questions, and we do our best to answer each and every one of them. We teach our techniques and share lots of valuable information. Once some of our members come to know, like, and trust me and our family, we can move them to step two.

Step two is to create an avatar for them. This entails getting the member to answer some questions that will identify the best path for them to take.

- What do you want to buy?
- What do you like to buy?
- What is your risk type and profile?
- What would it be best for you to invest in?
- In what state would you like to have investment properties?

• Do you prefer cash flow or depreciation?

Once we get to know you, your investment portfolio, and preferences, then we start to identify opportunities that best fit your profile. We generally have a couple of offerings in multi-family and a couple in commercial real estate—(NNN) triple net properties and storage and industrial.

You really need a variety of asset classes to keep growing and adding to your portfolio to mitigate risk. In our case, we own a lot of commercial real estate in the non-syndicated sphere (individual investments). We also own syndicated group projects where we buy assets together by purchasing NNN buildings, multi-family apartment complexes and storage/industrial. Right now, the interest rate is high and the cap rate hasn't quite caught up, so we are buying all cash.

Folks can't buy these NNN deals on their own right now. Let's say we are buying a Starbucks for three-million dollars. The cap rate is about 5.2 percent and the interest rate is up around 7 or 8 percent if you're borrowing from a local conventional bank. At this time, the cap rate would not supersede the interest rate, so you would be upside down if you tried to take a loan to purchase this. What we do is syndicate this investment with partners, usually 15 or 20 people who put in the amount that it takes to buy the property outright—cash—no loan! For ease of figuring this out in your head, think in terms of everyone putting in $100,000 each, or the amount needed divided by the number of investors to get to whatever the amount is needed to buy the property. The property will have no loan on it so every partner benefits from that property's cash flow starting day 1! The property starts to generate cash flow income immediately because of the lease in place via the highly-rated, corporate tenant who is paying monthly rent. Like I told you with the properties we sold to the REIT, the tenants are locked into a long lease with a corporate guarantee. Money is generated for the investors from this rent, day 1 after closing.

People say to me, "But Julie, aren't you just making you and your investor partners the bank?" Yeah, kind of, but this way there is no debt on the asset. We have full and outright control. We have capital preservation, plus we are accumulating appreciation, while generating a nice amount of cash flow for our partners. The cost segregation is about 20 to 30 percent, so you're not getting in this to eradicate your taxes, but you do get cash flow and appreciation and an upside on sale from the increase in rental NOI (Net Operating Income) coupled with a cap rate compression (again, we can sell at any time that makes the most money for the investors because we have absolute control). Because we pay the amount for the property in full, investors will make cash flow day 1.

Cap rates are slowly climbing, but they will likely come down after or during the next election (the market is speculating on that). Even at the same cap rate we have now, the rent bump will still be 10 percent or more. When that rent rate goes up, usually set for about five years from when we buy, the property becomes more attractive to buyers, making the selling price go up significantly from the price we bought at.

As I have said several times, the tenants are always a highly-rated, corporate-guaranteed entity, like Starbucks or

Chipotle, Auto Zones, O'Reilly, Dollar Stores, QSR (quick service restaurants), corporate childcare centers, and other attractive businesses. No matter what the business, all of these NNNs are responsible for absolutely everything. The only things we could be responsible for are negated in that the major maintenance issues that would be on us to remediate are things like needing a new roof or structural damage, generally caused by age. We only buy new construction directly from the developer, so we are under warranty. The buildings are new—they have new roofs. The cash is stable, the rent is set in stone and not based on proformas; therefore, the monthly cash is stable. The only thing that could be an issue would be something like a national disaster or if the corporate tenant folds. Even then, most of these leases include corporate guarantees, and we mitigate risk by buying them in cash, so we always have the value of the building and land to rely on. And we own the buildings outright, so even if the Starbucks in that building went under (God forbid!), which is very unlikely if you know how careful Starbucks is about choosing locations, we can get another tenant in the building pretty quickly.

Once we started doing all of this ourselves, we had a lot of people asking if they could buy triple net properties with us. Most people don't have a million dollars hanging around, and it's more like three million to buy one Starbucks or a Taco Bell. Back in the day, you would likely be able to buy a property like this with 20 to 30 percent or so down and make money. That's not true now. The debt doesn't pencil. To make this work, you really have to buy all cash. Putting in $100,000 or so a share means you own only a portion of the investment but with mitigated risk. This allows you to deploy less capital into each project, mitigate your risk, and create various streams of income from different asset classes.

There are many different types and ways to invest. It all depends on what you feel comfortable with putting your money into. The economy might be a challenge right now, but there are always opportunities to look at. You can get a good deal on a property when an owner decides they just can't manage it any longer. It's a matter of thinking about what's best for you.

The other thing we offer people to invest in with us, is the multi-family properties. The bonus depreciation is changing this year. The LTV—loan to value—has changed. The bank used to allow loans with 20 percent down. Now, we are looking at 65/35 or 60/40 or 50/50. The banks aren't willing to take on high-risk or highly leveraged loans in these markets. Best part is: bonus depreciation doesn't expire!

There are two kinds of investment partnerships. You can be a limited partner (LP) or a General Partner (GP). A limited partner is someone who is simply a passive investor. They don't do any of the work and for most people who own a business or are in a full time W2 job, they don't have the time or the tenacity to be the GP. Pretty much everyone we work with is an LP. They give us money and trust us to do what needs to be done to make more money. When you have a business, you don't need another business. These passive investors do this, most of the time, as a tax deferment to mitigate money earned off their tax bill from other passive income they may have coming in like sale leasebacks, Airbnb properties or other real estate they may have that pays out passive income. Investing in multi-family can eradicate some or even most of their passive income tax bill.

So, we are usually the lead GPs, or the co-GPS, for these commercial real estate purchases. Had we known more about this when we ran the schools, we would have absolutely done more of this as LPs. We were busy running multiple schools and a myriad of projects, so we didn't have the bandwidth to take on yet another career. But now, we are the GP in all of the deals we offer to our investors. Initially, we were just LPs, in fact up until just a few short years ago.

As GPs, we are doing the work. With the multi-family projects, as I said, I am a co-GP. I am not generally the person finding the properties, but we come in during the due diligence period or when the property is ready to get under contract. We buy value add Class B apartments. Each apartment, over time, will get the basic makeover; new carpet and/or tile, new appliances, and a fresh coat of paint. As each of those get finished, the rent goes up based on the renovation. For the first six to eight months, we are mostly working on the improvements. We will paint the exterior, landscape, renovate the lobby, upgrade the pool, the gym, maybe add some carports, a pergola or a dog park. We start by renovating any vacant apartments, and then when a tenant renews their lease, we can either move them into another apartment while we renovate or they can move into a new apartment that is already upgraded and done. Sometimes they take that opportunity to move into a bigger unit for more money, if one is available, or move into a completed one the same size. Everyone is on a different leasing schedule, so you go with the flow to meet the expected proforma.

For existing tenants, we create a gradual rent increase of 2 percent to a total of 8 percent over the entire hold period. New tenants moving in for the first time sign a lease at the new rent price. As we increase the rent for our current tenants, we are also increasing and adding value. This is the time when you can also get people to leave who may not be paying, who are causing problems and/or are in arrears on their rent. The main thing is, we are increasing the overall value of the property a great deal, which is great for our tenants, but also great for our investors when it comes time to sell the whole thing.

There are A, B, and C level properties, based on the amenities offered, location, age of the property, perks and amenities/benefits that are reflected in the rent costs. As mentioned previously, we like to buy B level value-add properties. They are generally nice, but they have room for us to create a lot of value add. We add new amenities like storage lockers, Amazon lockers for deliveries, laundry facilities, and even pet parks, which became super popular during Covid. Everyone adopted a pet and then wanted to get outside and play with them. We create better parking, like reserved parking areas or pergola parking covers.

Because this all takes time as we do the renos, it takes at least six months before investors see any return on their money, unlike with the NNN properties. In multi-family there's not really much cash flow—generally between 2 percent to 6 percent. The multiple is on sale/exit (longer-term). We hold on to most of them for about five years. When we do sell, the return on investment is predicted to be close to double the initial investment. It depends on the market, but typically our investors see 1.8 to 2x return on their investment. So, if they invest, let's say, $200,000, when we sell, they are predicted to receive around $380,000 on exit.

We do try to leave something for the next buyer, things they can do for a value add after they purchase from us. All properties need updating after ten years, and there will always be things to fix or improve on. But we try to make sure there are some things they can still do, like maybe adding hot tubs, grilling areas, and upgrading or adding a clubhouse. For example, we had one complex where for the first-level apartments, we were able to fence in the backyards like a townhome. That's the kind of added value that translates into increased NOI (net operating income). Those extra yards in that complex even faced the pool, so we were able to charge a premium for those limited number of apartments.

Another space we are invested in is storage facilities. We are not the GP in these projects, but we're learning a lot about what it takes to be the GP for these projects.

The GP does all the upgrades to the storage facility asset, then eventually flips it. Once the reno is done, we raise the rent on each unit. We go into the storage units and clean, paint, refresh, add a new gate/fence, put in climate control, new doors, locks, security, etc., as they become open. Once we make those significant improvements, we can double or close to double the rent per month for each storage facility unit. We have maybe 100 LPs, who are all investing anywhere from $60K to 1 million each. The interest cash flow on these is high and can be 13 percent to as much as 30 percent with the average being about 20-25 percent internal rate of return (IRR), and there is a high increase in profit when the properties are ready to flip and be sold. Cha-Ching!

Investing can be confusing. Bankers and financial advisors might tell you to put all of your money in one place, mainly into their portfolios. Diversifying our investments is key. Of course, you need to think about the risk. You're going to need to be creating a risk mitigation strategy while you're creating wealth. But you're not going to create instant wealth or legacy wealth by putting all your money in one place and certainly without taking on some risk. Wealthy folks don't save, they invest.

For example, say you take 100 grand and do a single-family house flip. That kind of project requires so much money, energy, and so much time, with the things you have to do to make that money. Why just single-family homes? Not that it's bad to flip a house, that's great, but you're never going to get to $50+ million dollars in real estate doing that. You're just not.

Knowing if you are a moderate, medium, or high-level risk taker can help you properly define your investment avatar. Questions to ask yourself might be: Are you interested in class A and new development properties? Are you more of an NNN standardized, consistently stabilized income investor? Do you want more value-add, renovation driven, extremely passive investments? Where are you and what makes sense for your return on life right now? This can be malleable. How much do you know about what you're investing in? Education will help determine where you are with the overall risk.

I'm big on talking about and working through the risk assessment questions with our clients first thing. People need to be aware of all sides: the good, the bad, and the ugly. If you think you're going to do any of this with no risk (opening a business, scaling your current business, exiting, or investing), or conversely that you're not going to do anything because of risk then you will not grow, period. This brings us right back to your mindset—scarcity to abundance, right? You can have a growth mindset, but if you don't take any action, or you don't appreciate the theory of decently calculated risk, you're still going to be in the same spot you were in when you started this book... or possibly worse off.

Even with the seeming ups and downs, cyclically, over the last 100 years, real estate is always on an up curve. It will go up and down and then up a little more. Property and land is finite. There is just so much of it, and someday there will be no more.

When I explained the investment program that we offer to investors, both of our parents said the same thing. "How can this work? Is it safe?"

I had a conversation with our parents. They were like, "Oh, my! So, if we give you $120,000.00 dollars, you're going to give us $571 a month, every month, for five years and then our money back, plus the appreciation?"

"Yes!" The interest rate on this investment is higher than the banks—5.71 percent and it goes to 7.2 percent if we keep the hold, and that's just cash on cash. That's not the appreciation. There's the appreciation on the property and regular 10 percent rent bumps for the tenant, which is Starbucks cafes.

This is hard for them to get. It was hard for us to get at first. We're not brought up with that kind of knowledge. We didn't know this kind of investment existed. If we did, we would have been doing this a hell of a lot sooner, I'll tell you that. Believe me, we regret not getting into this kind of investing much earlier. The good thing is that we do this for ourselves and lots of other people now. We love that we can give all this information back to our friends, family, and investor partners. My dad constantly says he wishes he would have invested in real estate sooner. We say the same thing. Every one of our investors says the same thing, too.

The old saying holds true: *Don't wait to invest in real estate. Invest in real estate and wait!*

ACTION ITEMS:

☐ Discuss with your accountant how much of your savings or income you can safely invest.

☐ Create an investment avatar. Start to make a list of the kinds of things that you would be excited to invest in.

☐ Work backwards. Do the exercise "Finding my Freedom number." Take what you need to live off and divide it by .04 percent (average amount, conservatively, you will make off your money's interest) to get a basic idea of what you will need to live without a W2 job or without an active business.

☐ Consider the benefits of investing in commercial properties, especially NNNs.

WHAT DOES THIS ALL MEAN FOR YOU?

S o, are you ready to start—or continue—building your empire? As you've learned from my experience, it's not merely about working hard or accumulating wealth. Building your empire begins with having a clear idea of your ultimate goal and then committing to achieving it. It requires overcoming entrenched attitudes about money, particularly if you were raised in a family with a scarcity mindset, and being willing to take calculated risks. It also takes surrounding yourself with supportive people—staffers, business partners, mentors, and family members—and not worrying about how others will judge you when you need to prioritize business over work (or vice versa).

Building your empire is about crafting a legacy that harmonizes between business and life. Scaling a business demands strategic thinking, unwavering dedication, and an unyielding commitment to innovation. Strategic exits, whether through mergers, acquisitions, or sales to private equity, can be the culmination of years of hard work, and they are opportunities to leverage the value you've built

Generational wealth, the ultimate aspiration, is about ensuring that your empire withstands the test of time, benefiting not just you but your descendants. It requires careful planning, financial acumen, and a focus on values that transcend the balance sheet. Don't be afraid to educate your kiddos about how they can build their brands and live a fearless life of potential—both in business and with family.

As you embark on your journey to empire building, remember that success is not measured solely in monetary terms. It's about the impact you have on the world, the lives you touch, and the lasting contributions you make. With the knowledge and insights gained from this book, may you pave your own path to success, leaving an indelible mark on the world and securing generational wealth for those who follow in your footsteps.

Be fearless—and have fun!

GLOSSARY OF TERMS

Throughout this book, I've touched on a lot of business and financial concepts and strategies that you might not be all that familiar with. Here are brief definitions of common terms and acronyms every entrepreneur and empire builder needs to know.

APY. Annual Percentage Yield. The real rate of return earned on an investment, taking into account compound interest.

CAPITAL GAIN. This refers to the increase in the value of an asset categorized as capital, such as a stock or property, when it is sold.

CPA. Certified Public Accountant

CRM. Customer Relation Management system

DBA. Doing Business As. Simply a name that brands your business.

DTI. Debt to Income Ratio

EBITDA. This stands for Earnings Before Interest, Taxes, Depreciation, and Amortization. It's a metric that evaluates the operating performance of a company—how much money the company is actually making is part of this metric.

FICO. An abbreviation for the Fair Isaac Corporation, the first company to offer a credit-risk model with a score.

GP. General Partner.

HELICOPTERING. A style of parenting where caregivers are highly involved in their child's life. Their intense focus can negatively impact a child's mental health, self-image, coping skills, and more.

INCOME TAX. A type of tax governments impose on income businesses and individuals within their jurisdiction generate. By law, taxpayers must file an income tax return annually to determine their tax obligations. Income tax is paid on earnings from employment, interest, dividends, royalties, or self-employment, whether it's in the form of services, money, or property.

IRA. Individual Retirement Account.

IRR. internal Rate of Return.

KPIS. Key Performance Indicators. Targets that help you measure progress against your most strategic objectives.

LLC. Limited Liability Company. A structure that establishes your business as its own distinct legal entity.

LOI. Letter of Intent. A document declaring the preliminary commitment of one party to do business with another.

LP. Limited Partner. In an investment agreement, an LP earns passive income.

MRR. Monthly Recurring Revenue. Used to measure what a company expects to receive monthly from customers for providing them with products or services.

NDA. Non-Disclosure Agreement. A confidentiality agreement used by companies in order to protect privileged information and sensitive information.

NNN. Triple net properties; a type of commercial real estate investment.

P/L. Profit and loss statement. Summarizes the revenues, costs, and expenses incurred in running a business.

REITS. A kind of mutual fund that buys real estate instead of putting the investor's money into stocks (pronounced REET).

ROFR. First Right of Refusal. In commercial real estate, an ROFR gives the investor the option to take over and fully control the tenant's business operation in a worst-case scenario.

ROTH IRA. Named after Senator Willam Roth, this IRA has fewer restrictions than a standard IRA. The main difference between Roth IRAs and most other IRAs is that qualified withdrawals from the Roth IRA are tax-free as well as growth in the account. Also, with a Roth IRA, you might have investments in stocks and bonds, securities, mutual funds and even real estate.

SBA. Small Business Administration.

SDIRA. Self-directed IRA. A type of IRA, managed by the account owner, that can hold a variety of investments.

SCALING. Beyond growing a business, scaling involves reproducing business operations and products to meet the demands of larger markets while focusing on increasing revenue.

SALE-AND-LEASEBACK. Or simply a leaseback. A financial transaction where the owner of an asset, such as a building, sells it and then leases it back from the new owner.

SOP. Standard Operating Procedure. A company's preferred or official way of implementing business policies.

UNIVERSAL LIFE. A permanent type of life insurance policy that typically has lower premiums than whole life.

ACKNOWLEDGMENTS

I would like to express my deepest gratitude to my husband, our four children, our parents, and our family for their unwavering support and encouragement throughout this arduous journey. Your love, patience, and understanding have been my anchor, allowing me to pursue my passion with determination and resilience.

To my mentors and advisors, thank you for your invaluable guidance and wisdom. Your insights have shaped my thinking and inspired me to strive for excellence in every endeavor.

A heartfelt thank you to my friends, peers, and colleagues for your encouragement and belief in my vision. Your words of encouragement and enthusiasm have been a constant source of motivation.

I am also grateful to the countless individuals who have shared their stories and experiences with me. Your openness and honesty have enriched this book and made it much more impactful.

I am also so grateful to the publishers (especially Lil Barcaski), the editors, proofreaders, and designers who worked tirelessly to polish and refine this manuscript. Your attention to detail and creative input have made this book shine.

Lastly, I want to extend my appreciation to the readers who have chosen to embark on this journey with me. It is my sincere hope that this book serves as a source of inspiration and empowerment, guiding you toward success and fulfillment in all aspects of your life.

Thank you.

Thanks and make it a great day!

ABOUT THE AUTHOR

JULIE ROY, a Canadian-born daughter of Italian immigrants and self-described "multi-million dollar mama," is driven by an unstoppable work ethic and passion for defying the ordinary. She takes pride in harmonizing her family with her work as an entrepreneur, investor, speaker, author, podcaster, and coach. Through her speaking engagements, coaching program, and real estate investment club, she helps entrepreneurs multiply their net worth, create passive income streams, and secure generational wealth in significantly less time than time than it would take to do it on their own.

Julie built her business empire through hard work, calculated risks, and learning from costly mistakes. In her early

20s, with no experience or mentorship, she took a $25,000 loan at 19 percent interest from a back-alley shark to start a Montessori preschool. She paid it off it a year, through sheer determination, but it took a decade to position her first business for a profitable exit. However, with strategic guidance and valuable lessons learned, her second business venture scaled to 12X the multiple in just three years. The next go-round was even faster.

The mother of four children ranging in age from 'tween to early 20s, she makes her home in Omaha, Nebraska, with her husband and business partner, Beau.

To learn more about Julie Roy and her mission, visit:

TheJulieRoy.com

Investingwiththeroys.com

www.ingramcontent.com/pod-product-compliance
Lightning Source LLC
Chambersburg PA
CBHW071145120626
46546CB00006B/2131